Waking Up Indigo

PERSONAL STORIES AND
PRACTICAL GUIDANCE
ON SPIRITUAL AWAKENING

Natha Jay

To my other
Natha —
I am so
blessed to have
your light in my
life + love,
Natha

To Maddie, Amy, and Gardner
Thank you for the foundation of
unconditional love,
and always allowing me to be me.
Best. Family. Ever.
May you rest peacefully in the Heart of Grace.

TABLE OF CONTENTS

Introduction

You are not alone.

When I was young (meaning the first three decades of my life), I had no context for my experience, no name for my group, and no idea there even was a group. I felt totally alone on this planet. It wasn't until I had a reading by a wonderful woman named Shikiah that I was given validation of my experience. She said, "Before we start this reading, I need to tell you you're an Indigo and you are not alone."

I had no idea what an Indigo was, but I broke down crying just hearing I wasn't alone. I went home and researched the term, and sure enough, something finally explained me. More importantly, there were enough of us to warrant an avalanche of information on the subject.

Instead of explaining Indigos, I attempt to explain being human. Most people understand the physical side, but when we incarnate, an ego is just standard issue. Navigating that piece can be challenging. I'm pretty sure the incarnation brochure read, "Be human! There's beer and chocolate and sex!" and it never mentioned the ego part. I try to explain its function, care, and feeding from my observations. The important stuff is interspersed with personal stories for your entertainment. Yes, they're all true.

This book is for us – the Indigos, the star children, the Lightworkers of all sorts. If you are drawn to this book, the Universe is beckoning you to remember who you really are, with the assurance you are not alone. And together we change the world.

"Take courage, friends.
The way is often hard, the path is never clear,
and the stakes are very high.
Take courage, for deep down, there is another truth:
You are not alone."
~ Wayne B. Arnason

AWAKENING

CHAPTER 1

∼ Talking to God ∼

I was four years old, playing with my dolls when it happened. My Grandma was doing laundry and singing to herself, when I had the sudden realization that everything was perfect, exactly as it should be, because I was here. At the same time, I understood that if I had never been born, everything would be just as perfect, but in a whole different way. Not exactly a normal epiphany for a child, or even most adults, but I understood it completely, and felt its truth in my very core. I thought *Oh good. Everything is perfect, I can go now.*

Having no idea where I should go, and using all the options available to a four-year-old, I put a dress on my dog, packed my doll in a play suitcase, and headed for the park. This was a very small town in 1976, and the park was only two blocks away. It really wasn't that daring of an adventure. Besides, where else would I go?

When I got to the park, I sat on a bench and wondered *what now?* A blinding, white light, and several "beings" immediately surrounded me. I assumed this was God, even though it seemed odd that God would appear as multiple and androgynous... but I supposed God could appear any way He chose. That's the prerogative of being omnipotent.

The communication that followed was a mixture of visions and meaning conveyed without a medium, like just knowing something without hearing or seeing it. The basic message was this: *Would you be willing to help us out? Your life wouldn't be as "fun" as a normal human life, but it would mean a lot to us.* Sort of take one for the team. I agreed, and asked what to do. They replied just keep your heart open. Then I experienced the crucifixion, the weight and pain of that life of service, emotional weight and spiritual weight. Then I felt the release from the body, and the incredible contrast of freedom and love as my spirit soared. Then it was over. Just like that. I was just sitting in the park.

As I got up and started my short walk home, my body felt so very heavy. I thought to myself *starting over is always such a bummer.* My mission has always weighed heavily on me. At the same time, I never felt special. It was years before I even told my Mom about my experience, because I thought everyone got a mission. In my mind, you learned to walk, then you learned to read, then you got your mission from God, then you started Kindergarten. I was four. Made sense to me. I was eight or nine when I started to realize not everyone was aware of having a mission, so I told my Mom about this experience and asked her if it was normal. Apparently not.

Almost forty years later, I still remember it like it was yesterday, but my interpretations have changed a bit. Instead of God, I think it was my guides contacting me. Instead of asking me to take on this mission, I think they were reminding me why I came. It has been the defining moment of my entire life, and my understanding of it expands and evolves all the time. But I do think the directive is exactly as they stated: *Just keep your heart open.*

"We can hear the silent voice of the spiritual universe within our own hearts."
~ Ruth St. Denis

"Sometimes the heart sees what is invisible to the eye."
~ H. Jackson Brown, Jr.

AWAKENING

This word has been floating around quite a bit for the past few years, but what does it really mean? What does a spiritual awakening look like? Well, you won't get a straight answer because they are all different, just as we are all different. They range from a shift in perspective to physical sensations; they can be gradual or sudden, pleasant or terrifying. The one thing they have in common is that you are different from that point on, forever changed.

The thing about awakening that seems to be overlooked is that it isn't a one-time occurrence. Poof! You're spiritually awakened! Well, yes, it certainly feels that way, at least until the next one hits. I had my first awakening when I was 4-years-old, before I had developed a real sense of self, so spirituality just naturally became part of my identity. This made my youth a bit of a struggle, but compared to those waking up later in life, I think it was the easy road. Adults spiritually awakening for the first time, after investing so much time and energy in building a worldly life, can be a traumatic experience, especially when it's sudden.

One of the most dramatic experiences is usually referred to as a Kundalini Awakening. It is usually characterized by physical tingling and heat, feelings of bliss and unity with all things, and the sudden ability to feel everyone around you (physical empathy), and these things last for hours or even days. That part is all well and good, but then you crash back down to this life and have to try to make sense of it all, along with integrating these new skills into your life. Functioning in this world as a new physical empath can be tough. It's a whole deal.

More common, is remembering you are here for a reason, a spiritual mission, or suddenly becoming aware you are more than your mind and body. Most of us theoretically believe we have a soul, but when it becomes a deep knowing it's just different than a mental theory. This will start you on a quest of self-discovery, a hero's journey, and trust me, you'll never get bored. "Know thyself" is the prime directive for the mystery schools for a reason.

At the moment (since 2012) the masses are experiencing a shift in perspective. People are no longer pacified by being fed misinformation, and being told how to think and feel. The world is beginning to question everything. Why are we here? What is money, really? Do we really need religion? Why is power not shared? It may seem small at this point, but awakening builds rapidly, especially now. The really important thing to remember is that this is happening to the majority of humans, not just a few of us anymore.

I have picked up a few tricks along the way for handling spiritual awakenings, and I hope you find them helpful to your journey.

Community – Find the others. You are NOT alone. The beauty of the Internet allows us to connect with others going through the same thing.

Daily Practice – Do something to feed your soul and empty your mind everyday. It doesn't matter if it's meditation, gardening, running, etc. You know what clears your mind, just make it a priority.

Unplug – Stop listening to the news, reading beauty magazines, and even asking your friends for advice. Spiritual growth is an inside job, and you need some peace and quiet to hear your own inner guidance.

Surrender – The only reason change is hard is because we cling to the past. The old you is gone, and fighting to get it back is where the suffering comes from. This process isn't something we can control, and it is guided by a higher power. Trust the path.

*"That is the real spiritual awakening,
when something emerges from within you that is deeper
than who you thought you were. So, the person is
still there, but one could almost say that something
more powerful shines through the person."
~ Eckhart Tolle*

*"To be fully alive, fully human,
and completely awake is to be continually
thrown out of the nest."
~ Pema Chodron*

SPIRITUALITY

Religion is crowd control. To be involved in a religion requires adherence to its dogma, in action, word, and deed (and usually dress). Religion requires a belief in someone else's experience, and discourages you having your own. It's about following rules, and coloring inside the lines. At best, religion points us in the direction of a higher power, at worst, it insists that higher power can only be reached through its methods or clergy, thus completely denying a personal connection with the Divine.

Spirituality, on the other hand, is a personal relationship with the Divine, without a middleman. Yes, you can be religious and spiritual at the same time, but it's not common. Why? Religion focuses outward for the answers (Holy books, messiahs, rituals), whereas spirituality focuses inward (be still and listen, know thyself). In spirituality we learn to determine right from wrong using our own inner moral compass, instead of following an external list of directives. If we all developed and relied on this internal compass, many interactions would be quite different. We all know war feels wrong, yet we follow orders of an outside source instead of listening to our own inner truth, primarily because that's what we've been taught.

Metaphysics are principles of reality that we currently have no way to measure. As science advances we will develop ways to measure subtle energy, and metaphysics will become physics. Quantum physics is well on its way to uniting the scientific and spiritual realms by studying, measuring, and documenting metaphysical principles.

Mysticism is like spirituality on acid. It takes the personal relationship with the Divine to a whole new level. After you've experienced even a glimpse, poems by Rumi and

Hafiz start to make sense in a whole new way. Words can't even approach the experience. I think mystical experiences just happen; there's not much you can do to encourage it, except maybe develop your own spirituality.

Developing your spirituality is like developing anything else - it takes time and commitment. No, this isn't about drudgery and discipline (that's religion), it's about developing a new relationship with your own soul. If you get a new puppy, take it home and play with it for a week, then just leave it in the backyard and ignore it, you will never have an actual relationship with that dog. If you spend time with it on a regular basis, care for its needs, and play with it, the relationship grows into a loving bond. Forming a relationship with the Divine takes your active participation, as does any relationship.

Active participation will look different to everyone, as we are all very different people. Maybe it's a silent prayer of thanks before each meal, maybe it's a long walk in the woods each week, maybe it's meditation three times a week, maybe it's a regular yoga class, maybe it's writing a gratitude list in your journal every night... there is no "right" way to connect, but you have to make time for it somewhere in your life. You must be present to win.

If it still seems daunting, start with your breath. Conscious breathing brings your attention inward, and reminds us that every breath is sacred. Try this: Inhale for 4 counts, hold the breath in for 4 counts, exhale for 4 counts, hold the breath out for 4 counts, repeat sequence for at least three minutes. If you take the time to breathe consciously a few times each day, your life will begin to shift. And if you do this three times a day you're setting aside time for this new relationship with the Divine. Best 9 minutes you'll spend all day. It doesn't take a huge amount of time, just a willingness to connect and grow.

HEALING

First of all, stop blaming yourself for every discomfort you may be experiencing. Stop blaming others, also. Just stop blaming entirely. True healing begins with acceptance and forgiveness. Radical forgiveness, all the way back to the original wound of separation from Source.

There is so much guilt and shame around illness, both physical and psychological. In our culture of blame, where accountability has come to mean only liability, our automatic response to disease is figuring out whom to blame. This simply blocks healing, even though it is generally our initial reaction, triggered by fear and conditioning. More often than not, the sick person eventually turns the blame inward, where it festers into shame and guilt, only worsening the condition. You don't live in a bubble, and we all share a (rather toxic) physical environment, so compassion and forgiveness are vital, especially toward oneself.

Then there are bloodlines. We know physical things are passed down genetically, like eye color, but there is new research showing genetic markers for psychological trauma passed down through generations. That irrational fear of needles I have? It may well be genetic, and have nothing to do with me thinking or feeling the "wrong" thing. Think about how many generations came before you, and the trauma some of those people endured, and unknowingly passed on in their DNA. Aside from behavioral conditioning, there is also a genetic component at work.

Then we go beyond the physical to the metaphysical. Entities, parallel timelines, alternate dimensions, all currently being examined by science, also have an effect. No need for details at this point, just know there's a lot more going on than we realize.

Disease isn't all about us, and it isn't all about now. While illness is not all your fault, healing all you can is absolutely your responsibility.

Accountability is really about personal power and free will. If diabetes runs in your family, you can either resign yourself to that fate, and enjoy doughnuts for breakfast everyday, or you can *choose* to eat properly and exercise to minimize the effect of the disease. You can also choose to look into the root beliefs, passed down genetically, which triggered its presence in your family. Doing this deeper work helps to clear the bloodlines for future (and past) generations. You have a choice. Free will is a thing. Use it to heal all you can.

Blame and resignation are the easy way out, but with courage, there are other options. We can use our free will to either perpetuate patterns of illness, or to heal them. We can be fully accountable to ourselves without judgment. The study of epigenetics shows us we have much more genetic fluidity than previously imagined, and also a much greater capacity to heal. Start where you are, forgive the past, and bring awareness to your future choices.

Don't get me wrong, you have an immense power and responsibility in your healing, but it's time to release the self-deprecating thought process that ultimately limits our progress. Radical forgiveness, unconditional love, and empowered free will... that's the best recipe I have for healing.

RELEASE

As you awaken it becomes obvious you need to release old patterns, old habits, old programming. Even a few years ago this was a tremendous process, involving deep emotional work, like psychotherapy, that may go on for years. Not much fun. Now, we have a greater understanding of the subconscious, and how to easily remove blocks to our progress. This doesn't alleviate the personal responsibility of being involved in the process, but it sure makes it easier.

Dr. Candace Pert has done some fabulous work to show us that our body is the subconscious mind. We tend to think of the subconscious as some abstract concept, with no clear mechanism of interaction, which controls our behavior without permission. It really isn't that mysterious - it's cellular memory. The question then becomes, how do we change it?

There are many techniques available to work with subconscious programming, like EFT, EMDR, and PSYCH-K. I will focus on PSYCH-K as I have much personal experience with it, being a practitioner for almost a decade. When I do a Core Belief Balance, which involves several basic subconscious programs changing at once, it usually has physical side effects within the first 12-24 hours after the balance. The most common is various levels of fatigue – anywhere from needing to lie flat for a few minutes to needing a six-hour nap. In a few cases, the side effects are more dramatic – flu symptoms, headache, vomiting, and diarrhea.

Why the disparity? Two reasons. First, how much, and what area, of their body is dedicated to holding these programs. Second, how well they can process the cellular release, or toxins. If their body is already so toxic that adding to the load is overwhelming, then illness results, at least temporarily. Whenever you release a subconscious program you are actually releasing chemicals on a cellular level. It is a physical detox process. Yes, to some extent, it can work the other way – doing a body detox and help release cellular memory. Doing both together is best.

That brings me to our current evolutionary situation (since 2012). As the vibration of the planet and human consciousness rise, we are all shedding old programming to make room for the new. This will be much easier on your body if it isn't already overwhelmed with toxins. Take care of your body, now more than ever, to make this a smooth transition. You don't need to do anything drastic, just start where you are. I recommend three days at a time, cleaning up your diet and lifestyle just a little. For example, do three days without fast food and soda, or three days without caffeine and alcohol. If you don't normally consume those things maybe do three days without meat, or without sugar, or three days of only veggie juice. If you need to move more, do three days of walking around the block, or morning yoga. Just start where you are, and make a small change for three days. If something feels good, keep doing it.

If you can't make a change for three days, you may need to put some thought into what addiction looks like, and how limiting it is. Addiction keeps us stuck by holding that cellular memory in place. If you "need" some substance, just be aware that it is keeping certain cellular functions switched off, and unable to release. Even PSYCH-K isn't nearly as effective when there are foreign substances in the way, including prescription drugs. Awareness is everything. Just being aware of this connection between addiction and cellular retention may help break the cycle.

This takes care of the subconscious, which is where so many get stuck, but release of old beliefs, trauma, and programming also involve conscious effort. Like I said, this isn't nearly as much effort as it used to be, but it takes conscious participation. Awareness. Again, start where you're at and take baby steps. The goal, which possibly no one has yet reached, is to be aware of every breath you take, and the energy it moves in your body. I ain't there, but it's good to have a goal!

Maybe start by studying some basic psychology, so you understand things like projection and codependency. Then study the ego and how we create our experience through it. Question your own beliefs, observe your own thoughts, and understand your personal self-limiting behaviors. Many things will release just by bringing them into your awareness, and if you get stuck, use one of the techniques to adjust the subconscious, and release cellular memory.

Sounds simple, and it's much easier than it used to be, but constant awareness is exhausting at first. How much time do we spend checked-out? Television, drinks with friends, zoning out while driving, listening to the monkey mind babble... we don't normally spend much time being fully present. This part of the process requires your dedication. No one else can do this part for you. Are you ready for the journey?

"Some of us think holding on makes us strong;
but sometimes it is letting go."
~ Hermann Hesse

Funny, how my Guides leave out all the details. When I agreed to "take one for the team" by living a life that wouldn't be "as fun" as human lives usually are, no one mentioned anything about a degenerative neurological disorder. Apparently, they have spin-doctors on the other side.

As I walk down the concourse pulling my flight case behind me, I stumble, yet again, on nothing in particular. I think to myself: *Shit. I have to think about every step or else I trip. It has to be obsessive-compulsive disorder. I'm as crazy as Howard Hughes.* Both my Mom and Grandma had mental breakdowns in their 20's, so at 28, I had good reason to question my mental health.

At the time, I was working as an airline pilot, and keeping the required medical certification meant visits to my aviation doctor every six months. These medical screenings are pretty thorough, and completely unforgiving of mental illness. It took me several months to get up the courage to see someone about the issue, and when I did they said, "Probably a brain tumor. We'll set up an MRI." What? Who says that? A least a brain tumor seemed more bearable than insanity. I've always been rather fond of my mental function.

After six months of poking and prodding, I was given a genetic test that confirmed the diagnosis of Friedreich's Ataxia. I got to keep my mental function, and be fully cognitive of my slow physical degeneration. Nice. Needless to say, that was the end of my brief flying career, and the beginning of a complete redirection of my life. I wouldn't recommend the disorder, but having it has afforded me the luxury of an entirely new relationship with myself, both body and soul.

As usual, I had a little forewarning, which I completely

misinterpreted. During the three months prior to going to that first doctor, my guides kept repeating, "walk away." I would always respond with what seemed to me to be reasonable arguments: I have invested too much time and energy into flying to just walk away from it, I can do whatever you need AND my career; it's my life and I want to be a pilot; and finally ending with a simple 'no'. Refusing to walk away and then losing my ability to walk seemed like a cruel and unusual punishment, but definitely a punishment.

I felt such a deep betrayal, from both God and my own body. I didn't speak to my guides for almost two years after that. I have decided that Hell is actually that willful disconnection from a Higher Power. They never left me, I left Them. I would cry and curse and throw tantrums about how unfair this was, and They would just be there, silently holding the space, waiting for me to return. During that time, my physical condition deteriorated rapidly, as I was actively blocking Source energy. Once I realized this, and burned out most of the anger, I opened up to Them again. I still cry thinking of that reunion, so loving and tender.

Shortly after that I decided my efforts were best spent exploring alternative healing. During one of my first quests, I went to see a woman for some energy work, and ended up also getting a reading. Apparently, my guides were pretty insistent on getting me a message. They said this condition wasn't a punishment, I had done nothing wrong, and it was going to happen no matter what. The message to "walk away" was to try to make the transition less painful; it wasn't an ultimatum.

This was possibly the greatest healing I have ever received, because it was the beginning of healing the deep betrayal I felt, healing my relationship to both my body and soul. I've come to realize that is the fundamental healing we are all searching for. No matter what the situation, we want to know we didn't do anything wrong, we aren't being punished, and we just want to be whole.

For the next decade I learned several types of energy work, experimented with innumerable alternative healing modalities, and studied countless spiritual texts. Know Thyself was my insatiable mission. Yoga retreats, Merkabah training, I was even ordained as an Interfaith Minister after two years of seminary. More spiritual adventures than I can count.

About now you would expect me to say 'I just never gave up', but that isn't how I work. I gave up on a regular basis - I just didn't stay there. I always managed to pull myself back up and keep going. If I'm anything it's resilient, because I gave up a lot. I just don't see exhaustion as failure, so I could crash, let it pass, and move on. It isn't pretty, but it works for me.

About a decade in, I got the clear message I needed to clear my family bloodlines, and after about two years of that, I got that I was helping to clear all bloodlines. Well, that would have been some nice information to have at the beginning of all this! My Guide's response: *Really? It would have been better to tell you the next 15 years of physical degeneration and suffering are just part of the plan, and there's nothing you can do to help yourself. Have fun with that.* Well, yes, I see your point. At least I kept myself busy learning new and useful things.

Then in May of 2013 I felt my DNA change. Don't ask me to explain that one, I've just always had a very open relationship with my body. I've had whole conversations with my liver. It makes sense in my world. Since then, I've shown slow but steady improvement. Suddenly, new healers and alternative technologies started popping up around me, all proving quite beneficial.

As of March 2015, the changes are impressive. The latest thing I've learned is that spontaneous remission is a lot of work. Rebuilding muscle and relearning to walk is more painful than you would think and takes enormous amounts of energy and concentration. No wonder toddlers spend most of their time crying and sleeping... Now, instead of giving up, I just take a nap.

"What do you do when life blindfolds you and spins you around? We think it's our fault, that we're to blame, when really we should be focused on being gentle with ourselves."
~Melody Beattie

"The practice of forgiveness is our most important contribution to the healing of the world."
~ Marianne Williamson

YOUR MISSION

Like so many others, I spent many years trying to figure out what I wanted to be when I grew up, what vocation would fulfill my purpose in this life. After a very lengthy search, I found my calling, and I'll even tell you how to find yours.

Why are you here? What should you be doing? Ready??? You aren't here to DO, you're here to BE. A bit anticlimactic, isn't it? That can't be right... I feel the weight of this really important mission... *Well, you are your mission.*

As a collective, we are here to assist in the shift, to help raise human consciousness. Increasing the vibration, letting in more light, raises consciousness, and that is done through an open heart. When you are in an open, happy place, love just flows through you, and love changes the world. No, not just in a cliché way, it actually changes the vibration of the energy around you, and adds to the collective. All good things come through an open heart, and everyone brings in their own "flavor" of light.

Don't get me wrong; there is a lot of doing involved in being. Sitting on the couch, watching television, and eating ice cream isn't being, so much as just a lack of doing. Doing is essential to the process, but it just isn't the end goal, as we've always been taught. Proper diet and exercise are great things to *do,* in order to be more comfortable in your body. Meditation is something to do to *be* more balanced in your mind. Working is what we *do* to afford to live and *be,* and if your chosen career allows you to, even occasionally, open your heart, then it's a perfect place for you.

Only you know what career path assists you in opening your heart. And we often put the cart before the horse on this one... the job (or relationship, or financial state, or whatever you're chasing) is never the reason for your happiness; it can only encourage or discourage your openness. If you get an openhearted sense of gratitude and child-like jubilation when you successfully repair something, then choose a career where you can experience that regularly. It's the openness, the happiness of being, that's the goal here. You are here to live in that space as much as possible.

My career took some unexpected turns, and I wound up working as an aircraft dispatcher for almost a decade. The job itself didn't do much for me, but I was able to find ways to make it serve my higher good. I volunteered for various odd jobs in the department, including some teaching, and also became involved in the union. In addition, I was able to enjoy many a philosophical conversation with my co-workers, and take breaks outside in the sunshine. The key for me was to focus on the things that allowed me to be more fully myself, not on the nuts-and-bolts of a desk job. When I finally figured this out and really started to love my job, I knew it was allowed to shift. About a year later the company moved and I was laid-off. This opened up new opportunities and new adventures.

Jobs, relationships, and all things in life, have cycles, ups and downs. Sometimes things are going along great, and other times it's a real struggle. Just because it sucks sometimes, doesn't mean you're in the wrong place or doing the wrong thing. For me, rough times generally indicate I've lost sight of the point; I'm all wrapped up in doing and forget that it's all about being. When in doubt, I get quiet and check-in with my heart. It knows what it needs to be open, and it's usually just a change in perspective.

PERSONAL POWER

Power can never be taken, only given.

This is about personal power, a discussion of human psychology. Don't confuse this topic with physical or psychic attack. This will only address the psychological side of recovery and daily living.

Our society has engrained victimization so deeply, that most of us don't even have a reference to what personal power looks like. We all have good days and bad days; we all retreat into blame at some points. It is through awareness that we escape the programming, and find the ability to act instead of react. The more awareness we bring to our lives, the more power we cultivate. Victim mentality simply gives power away, while manipulators find a sense of power from convincing others to give up their own. The exchange is always voluntary, if unconscious. Bringing our behaviors to light is what's needed to allow for change.

Personal power is the ability to own your thoughts, take complete responsibility for your actions, and see life as a series of choices.

When we play the victim role, blame is the focal point. "It's his/her fault" "the government did this to us" "if those people would just straighten up"... including self-blame "I can't help the way I am" "I've never been good at this" "I'm not good enough." Every time a situation is out of your control and you feel like life is just happening to you, you are in victim mode. Yes, lots of things happen outside of our control, but we **always** get to choose how we think and act. The initial trigger just happens, but pausing before you act is where power lives. *Consciously creating the story you replay in your head is the greatest act of power, and will change the course of your life forever.* That may seem like a bold statement, but it's worth trying, isn't it?

Your self-talk defines your personal power, because our stories are the boxes we live in. It's the job of the ego to maintain the story we've chosen, even if it is chosen subconsciously. These stories are changeable, with the awareness to do so. Awareness is the key, without it we are destined to repeat old patterns at every turn. Humans are creatures of habit, and would generally prefer to stay the course, no matter how bad it is, rather than change. In addition, awareness takes focused attention, and then change is definitely more effort than most are willing to put in. This is why it usually takes a crisis (death of a loved one, serious health issues, etc.) to motivate people into awareness.

Addiction is the ultimate victimization. Addiction can involve any substance or behavior, and always includes some form of guilt or shame. Addiction is different in every case, but the first step out is to choose something different, to choose to get help. I would also venture to say the process of recovery is aided by removing guilt at every opportunity. Instead of feeling too weak to say no, simply change the situation to an empowered choice. "I choose to do this." Once you own it, you can change it. "Last night I made a choice I didn't like, " instead of "I failed, and now I hate myself." Remove the negative emotional response, and it leaves room for empowerment.

Personal power is a matter of radical personal responsibility.

How do you begin the process of empowerment?
First, evaluate your life. Find what areas and circum-

stances make you feel empowered or disempowered, then figure out why. Why do you feel disempowered in certain areas? It will always involve a sense of lack of choice.

Second, change the script. Look at how your self-talk in that area can be changed to an empowered choice. Instead of "I have to keep this awful job because I have bills," try "This job allows me to pay my bills, so I choose to keep going."

Third, stay aware. Be aware of your inner dialog, and be willing to change it whenever necessary. To be empowered you must be willing to take control of your thoughts. As your awareness grows, you begin to take responsibility for your actions, your words, your thoughts, and even your energy. When you reach the level of taking responsibility for how your very energy affects the world around you, you are ready to take the next step into esoteric power. This process takes time and dedication, but being truly empowered is a rare and wonderful thing.

*"Heroes are made by the paths they choose,
not the powers they are graced with."*
~ Brodi Ashton

FAST TRACK

You have only one job on the road to spiritual awakening: Make room. Spirit yearns for us just as much as we yearn for Spirit. Instead of chasing the Light, simply clear out the dark and the Light will fill the space. Shadow work (ego work) is our only job, and everything else just flows naturally.

The amazing part is the lengths people will go to simply to avoid ego work. It's impressive. Everything from addiction, to denial, to spiritual bypassing, all in an effort to maintain the illusion of self. The body wants to live, but also accepts death. The ego, on the other hand, won't even consider death, and will pull every dirty trick around to stay in complete control. You are NOT your ego, you are the observer. Your ego works for you, not the other way around - as long as you remain aware. Know Thyself. Know your ego's tricks, and it no longer controls you.

Avoidance, in its many forms, is essentially an unwillingness to be fully present and aware. Granted, this is a skill, and takes practice, since most of us weren't taught by example as children. Still, it is completely possible to learn at any age, with willingness and dedication, as with any new skill. Being fully present and aware also requires you to fully feel emotion as it occurs, and to take full responsibility for your actions. Two more things people aren't accustomed to. Many people have seen far enough past the boundaries of the ego that they run toward the Light. This has created an interesting phenomenon called spiritual bypassing. Basically, these folks try to go straight from initial awareness (just waking up) to enlightenment, without wading through the muck of the ego on the way. Please don't do this. It's a waste of your time, and it's really annoying to those actually doing the work. More importantly, it always backfires. You can develop a "spiritual ego", which only adds to the ego work when it all comes crashing down like a house of cards.

How do you know if you're really doing ego work? It's messy. It's terrifying, it's humbling, and it isn't any fun. As you get better at it, the processing gets faster, but it still sucks. So why would anyone want to do it? Well, the more ego stuff you remove, the more room you make for the Light to fill. This allows your frequency to raise, your body to heal, and Love to occupy every cell. Ultimately, this results in your Higher Self being able to descend into your body. True Divine Union.

The first step is always awareness. I'm not saying you can never take a night off again, I'm simply saying be aware and be honest with yourself. "I'm feeling overwhelmed, and consciously choose to have a glass of wine and watch a movie" is totally different than just always having wine with dinner to "wind down." Numbing out (by any means) is something we all do, but you may be surprised how often you do it, once you really observe yourself. Stop justifying, stop denying, and really own your every action. It's empowering... after the initial shock. Once you own it, you can change it.

Once you have glimpsed into the hold your ego has, it's time to get to work. Everyone is different and will be best served by a different path, just be sure the one you choose really works with the ego, instead of bypassing it. There are many options, from psychotherapy to support groups, and tons of valuable books on the subject. Just pick a path, and get to work... on yourself.

You have one job.

~ Sister Twin Flame ~

After I lost my medical and could no longer work as a pilot, I had to decide what I wanted to do for a living. I still had a job in aviation, but it's just not the same as flying. Great view.

Over several months, I narrowed it down to some form of counseling. It's something I do naturally; I just lack the formal training. After months of Internet research, I found a tiny, little ad in the back of a magazine for The New Seminary (TNS), and its spiritual counseling program. It was an Interfaith (think ANY faith) Seminary, and had no specific religious affiliation, so I could get past the word 'seminary'. As I wondered why I was drawn to this particular program I heard *it's not the material, it's the people.* Works for me.

TNS was located in New York City. It was a two-year program that could be completed by distance, except for two on-site retreats, which happened at the end of each year. The retreats were scheduled right after the last class of each year, so corresponding students could come a day early and enjoy a class in person. I did just that, and found out why I was drawn there.

As I walked up to the still locked door, someone stepped out from the shadows and said, "Hi! My name is Adriane." As is normal in introductions, I held out my hand, said, "I'm Natha," and made eye contact. That's when reality took a swift turn towards the twilight zone. When our eyes met, I saw my own soul looking back at me. *Oh shit. This isn't right. How can she have my soul? Is that even possible?* Then it was just awkward. What do you say to someone you know intimately, but have only just met? That whole day was odd. It felt like I was being drawn to her and repelled at the same time. Beautiful and terrifying. Okay, mostly terrifying.

The next day we started the retreat, and by day two people were commenting on our connection. "How nice you can be here with your sister!" "How long have you been best friends?" It was a shock to everyone that we had just met. It was definitely a shock to me.

In the four days of the retreat I ran through the gamut of typical twin flame emotions, though I didn't realize that's what was happening. My life usually works like this: Twin flames? *That sounds like a crock, I'm not buying it. Oh shit, I guess it's real... maybe I should read up on it.* So after I read about it, the whole thing made more sense, in a twilight zone kind of way. Even though there was no sexual attraction, I still experienced the overwhelming love, jealousy, feeling inadequate, and giddy elation that meeting a twin produces.

In all my research on the subject, the two things that don't fit are 1) the assumption that a person can only have one twin flame, and 2) that it always has a sexual attraction. Both false. I know of others who have more than one twin flame, and there are a few channeled books describing the soul as being built to incarnate in about half a dozen different people at a time.

Adriane and I live in different states, and parting at the airport was one of the most painful things I've ever experienced. It felt like part of my heart was being ripped out. We hadn't talked about the experience, and I didn't know if it was just me, or even if I would ever see her again. Over the years, we've become much closer, and visit in person at least once or twice a year. I still cry every time we part. I don't imagine that will ever change.

Since then, I've grown to know her as a friend, as well

as a twin. We also developed a telepathic link. For several months, we would talk telepathically daily, and then verify the information by phone about once a week. We know when the other is in distress, and we can help each other energetically. We also have the same strange things happen at the same time, so I can always rely on her for a reality check. She's amazing. I don't know how I managed to make it all those years without her.

The twin flame thing is real, and it is just as amazing and strange as advertised. In fact, it was at the very top of my "weird shit" list for years... until I found my second twin...

"I think on some level, you do your best things when you're a little off-balance, a little scared. You've got to work from mystery, from wonder, from not knowing."
~ Willem Dafoe

"Sell your cleverness and buy bewilderment."
~ Jalal ad-Din Rumi

TWIN FLAMES

We need to start with a couple definitions, since everyone has their own take on these terms.

Soulmate – A separate soul who incarnates with you on a regular basis, like friends hanging out. They can have any relationship to you: parent, child, friend, family, lover, and you meet several in your lifetime.

Twin Flame – Someone who shares the same soul. They can have any relationship to you: parent, child, friend, family, lover, and you have more than one, although you may not meet any in this life.

As we begin our ascension process, we are each shedding layers of the ego, allowing us to live more in tune with our soul. As we vibrate closer to our soul frequency, we are attracting others with a similar frequency, this is our soul family. Most of us have soulmates in our life, though we may not recognize them, and twin flames are starting to pop up all over. It used to be quite rare to meet a twin, but they are essential to the process we're in.

Soulmates are a support, and help us to deal with our emotional stuff. They are usually fairly smooth relationships, but also involve a fair amount of mirroring – they show us what we need to work on. That's just never fun, no matter what kind of relationship you have. Soulmates help us to grow, and work with our ego. We may have someone in our life for years before they play their part as a soulmate, or you might just "click" right away.

Twin flames are completely different. Think of a soul like an octopus with eight legs; it is a single, whole and complete creature, but it can move each leg independently. Many of us have about half a dozen other people on the planet right now sharing our soul. Your soul isn't broken, it's just gaining different experiences by incarnating as different people at the same time. These people are often radically different, living almost in polarity of each other, presumably for the variety of experience. During any other time in history those separate pieces wouldn't meet, but this mass ascension is calling for some powerful energy. I know a few people who have met two or even three twins.

There is some useful information out there, by people who have obviously had the experience, but I disagree with two major points they promote as fact: you have only one twin flame, and it must be a romantic relationship. There are twins where one of them is gay. Some twins try to have a romantic relationship and fail. There are twins whose age disparity is so great they aren't sexually attracted. I personally have a twin who is obviously my sister, not a lesbian lover. I know a couple of people who have met more than one twin, and have a very different relationship with each. Every set is different, and the Universe is much more mysterious than we imagine. Twin flame relationships are each unique, and can't be fit into a standard definition. The love is the same regardless of the relationship, and love is the whole point.

The twin flame phenomenon has gotten completely distorted in some circles, and become a kind of New Age "someday my prince will come" thing. I think this is due to people who have never had the experience trying to explain a spiritual awakening through psychology. Rumi would be medicated and locked up today for his ecstatic joy. This isn't a 3rd dimensional thing and can't be explained in that way. Yes, it's all about love, but not in the way we normally categorize that experience.

The concept of love we normally deal with is conditional love: I love you IF... (you behave the way I want, you fulfill some need of mine, etc.). The love twin flames share is completely unconditional, it's more of a vibration than an emotion, and it grows and expands, almost taking on a life of its own, which is why it is essential at this time. The object of their game is to transcend the ego, and return us all to the unconditional love of the Divine.

This is quite a challenge while we're still living in the 3rd dimension with our egos intact. Having a "normal" relationship with a twin is totally impossible, because that just isn't how it works. While a soulmate teaches us to work through the ego by mirroring, a twin teaches us to transcend the ego through triggering. Mirroring reflects our issues back to us, while triggering is caused by opposite traits needing to be incorporated and balanced. It is about lessening the polarity of our existence by integrating these opposite extremes.

There is also an element of choice in a soulmate relationship. When you are feeling overwhelmed by the mirroring of your ego, you can either work through that issue with that person, or move to a different soulmate and repeat the process until you learn whatever you need to learn. That's why so many people keep repeating the same type of relationship, trying to avoid their own ego. In my experience, twins are not a choice, they just happen. It's like a spiritual promotion to learning about higher dimensional relationships. Also, you can't leave. You can do the "runner" thing and pretend you have control over the situation, but twins bond on an energetic level, so once they find each other, they are never really apart.

Another reason twins are usually painted in a romantic light is that we simply don't have words to accurately describe the experience, and love is a pale comparison, yet it's probably the closest word we have. Blissful and terrifying, the comfort of returning home, seeing and being seen on a soul level, feeling completely exposed yet completely accepted. It's the most surreal and transformation experience I've ever had, but it isn't for everyone, the intensity can be overwhelming.

It is a Divine calling to accelerate personal growth, not a way to fill a personal void. If you're looking for a twin to complete you, just know that isn't at all what it's about. Soul based relationships are still relationships, whether working with the ego or transcending it. Anytime you are dealing with other people there will be "stuff" to work through. There is no "perfect match" that you will never fight with, but the work is kind of the point. So read all the fabulous twin flame info on the Internet and feel the love they are trying to convey, but remember twins are a matter of spiritual calling, not desire fulfillment. Opening and expanding the heart is what it's all about.

"Being deeply loved by someone gives you strength, while loving someone deeply gives you courage."
~ Lao Tzu

INTUITION

CHAPTER 2

~ MY POOR MOTHER ~

Raising an Indigo Child is always an adventure. They are strong willed, way too smart, opposed to authority, and incredibly psychic. When asked why she didn't want more children, she would reply, "One is enough," and she meant it. She still enjoyed it, and told me that when I decided to incarnate, she jumped at the chance to be my Mom. She was a mystic in her own right, and I am grateful to have had her guidance.

She used to occasionally attend a meditation circle, and I was allowed to accompany her, provided I would draw and color quietly while they were in session. Worked for me – the energy was fabulous, everyone was quiet, and I never had trouble entertaining myself. After a few of these sessions, I had to ask why the teacher dressed so poorly.
Me: "Why does Dee always wear purple and green? Doesn't she know they clash?"

Mom: "She wasn't wearing any green, only purple."

Me: "No, she always wears that green shall."

Mom: After thinking for a moment, "That wasn't clothing. I think you're seeing her aura."

Me: "Oh. It still clashes. Someone should tell her."

I was about 5.

One of my Mom's friends had one of those creepy, old houses with the staircase that takes you right to the center of the upper floor. To the right was my destination, to my left, in the very end room were a pair of glowing red eyes. Not cool. When we went home I told my Mom about the eyes. She said, "It doesn't surprise me. Kasey uses her Ouija board in there, and I'm sure she's not careful with it. Just don't go in there." Done. I was 6-ish.

When I was 4 I received my spiritual mission, which is a whole story by itself, but I thought it happened to everyone. Several years later, I started to realize not everyone was given this kind of direction. I hadn't shared the experience because I didn't know it was unusual. When I shared it with my Mom, and asked her if other people were given their mission, she just got all pale and shook her head. Huh. Who knew? I was probably 8 or 9.

After we moved into our new house, I invited a couple friends for a sleepover. Typical tweens, there was giggling, and screaming, and ghost stories. But the thing was, we could hear the ghost walking in the attic. We named him Harry. In the morning we told my Mom about Harry, and his footsteps. She got all faint and had to sit down. Apparently the old man who had lived there, and recently died there, was named Harold. He was around the whole time we lived there, pacing in the attic, and rattling the closet doorknob. I slept with a knife and a bible for a couple years. When I was 16 my Mom and I were on a long road trip. It

was night, she was driving, and I was asleep in the back-
seat. Out of a sound sleep, I sit up and shout, "Watch out for
the rabbit!" It sounded like this:
Me: "Watch out for the rab—"
thump *thump*
Mom: "Damn it! Too late, go back to sleep."
I went right back to sleep. This was just our normal by then.

Ah, the joys of raising an Indigo. This is only a small
sample of the trauma my Mom endured during my child-
hood. I feel incredibly blessed and eternally grateful to have
had such an amazing friend and guide as my Mom. May
your soul rest peacefully and your light shine eternally,
Mom. Maddie Robertson 1946-2010

"All that I am, or hope to be,
I owe to my angel mother."
~ Abraham Lincoln

INTUITION

People tend to wrap intuition, psychic abilities, and energy sensitivity in a shroud of mystery, usually laced with fear and intrigue. This makes for great TV, but it's just not helpful to those who are trying to understand or develop these skills. I tend to lean the other way and take a very analytical approach to extrasensory perception. It will all be explainable by science, once we develop instruments capable of measuring subtle energies.

First, we need to discuss how we process information. We use our 5 basic senses (sight, hearing, touch, smell, and taste) as an interface to understand the world around us. This information comes into our brains through either direct contact or what we call imagination. There are endless studies showing that the brain treats both methods identically, which is the power behind visualization. The brain fires the same neurons, releases the same chemicals, for both the real deal and the imagined image. Want proof? The simplest example, if not a bit crude, is the sexual fantasy. Your body reacts the same way if your partner is physically present as it does with an imagined liaison.

Next, we need to get comfortable with the imagination. This takes practice, and you will naturally be more adept with some senses than others. Let's start with a rose. Close your eyes and visualize a rose. Add as much detail as you can. Then begin to add in other senses: How does it smell? Can you feel the petals? The thorns? Spend some time with this image, and really explore your senses. Then try this with an orange, or cinnamon tea, or petting the cat. As I said, this takes practice, so try a few different images each day and see what happens.

Now we get to the good stuff... there are two ways the

imagination is activated: by creating with the mind, and by the intuition. What does that mean? I'm glad you asked! If you are actively thinking about imagining a rose, then you are creating that experience yourself. If you are minding your own business, getting groceries or cleaning the house, and the image (visual, smell, whatever) of a rose pops up by itself, then it is intuition that put it there. *The only difference between intuitive people and non-intuitive people is how they react to this unexpected information*: Non-intuitives justify this experience, while intuitives simply accept it with curiosity. The difference sounds like this: Non-intuitives say, "I must be thinking about a rose because I saw some in my neighbor's yard yesterday," while intuitives say, "A rose? I wasn't thinking about that at all. I wonder what that means."

Intuitive people are open to accepting an experience with wonder and curiosity. Non-intuitive people have to justify their experience.

You can see the appeal of justifying an experience. We are conditioned to believe it is necessary to control our thoughts, and that we are solely responsible for anything that happens in our mental process. It can be terrifying to accept that things can appear in your brain without you putting them there. Kind of a control freak's worst nightmare, really. It's so much more natural, at least in this society, to justify a thought or feeling than it is to accept that you're experiencing something you didn't generate.
So how do you strengthen your intuition? Awareness. Trust. Practice. It takes time to build this muscle of intuition. Practice using your imagination, and be aware of your thoughts so you notice when something unexpected

slips into your awareness. The more you work with it, the stronger it gets.

*"It is always with excitement that I wake up in the morning wondering what my intuition will toss up to me, like gifts from the sea.
I work with it and rely on it. It's my partner."*
~ *Jonas Salk*

"The only real valuable thing is intuition."
~ *Albert Einstein*

EMPATHIC ABILITIES

Empathic abilities are actually quite natural for humans, but as with most things natural, they have been trampled on and discouraged at every turn. Ideally, we would have been raised in a calm, safe, loving environment, encouraged to feel, and given tools to manage our energetic inputs. Instead, most people come from a dysfunctional, if not abusive, household, where it was painful and unsafe to feel, then labeled as oversensitive or moody. Many strong empaths end up in addiction, due to the need to numb out, or being medicated to be able to function in our chaotic word. All we really need is a little training on how to use the superpower we have.

What is an empath? They feel... everything. Their stuff, your stuff, the pain of the world. It's overwhelming, to say the least. They may enter a room and feel someone's headache, or someone else's broken heart. They can feel the good stuff, too, but humans tend to put most of their energy into projecting the bad. They don't just sense these things, they actually feel them in their bodies, so they tend to assume it's their stuff, because we are taught that we only feel our own feelings. This is why empaths so frequently get the moody label – because we all assume it's their stuff, too.

There are three tools all empaths need: awareness, shielding, and releasing.

First, be aware of your own energy, your own thoughts and feelings, and when they change, ask why before you own it. If you were feeling happy before you entered a group, and now you feel angry, don't just assume it's yours, question it. If possible, ask the group, "Which one of you is angry?" Sometimes people won't own up to it, but just asking the question shifts their mood. Empaths must always be aware of their own energy in order not to be swept up by others. Question every shift. Sometimes I am alone and will feel the collective shift. Sometimes it's hard to tell what's mine and what isn't. But it helps immensely to be aware of my own energy, and to question the changes.

Second, empaths need to develop, and regularly practice, an energetic shielding technique. I ground down into the Earth, and up into the Sun, and surround myself with a bubble of light. Empaths should do some similar visualization morning, night, and before going into any group. If I go out with friends, we always remind each other to "bubble-up" before we get to our destination. This energetic shielding works like a condom – you can still feel, but it offers a layer of protection. Don't think it will insulate you from feeling everything, it just helps to keep your energy separate, and it makes it easier to tell what isn't yours.

Third, develop and practice some form of releasing technique. It could be draining all foreign energies into the Earth (Gaia uses it like compost, so it doesn't matter if it's "negative" energy), or calling Archangel Michael to use his sword of fire to cut all cords, or standing in the violet flame of St. Germaine to burn away all that isn't in your highest good. Every night, and as needed during the day, clear yourself. As this becomes a daily practice, you will actually feel lighter when you clear. Funky energy will hang onto you for as long as you are willing to carry it, even if the willingness is subconscious. Releasing needs to be a conscious act.

As humanity awakens, more and more people are becoming empathic. It is a gift of our true nature, not a reason to hide under the bed (though it feels that way sometimes).

If we can start training ourselves, sharing our discoveries with our friends, and ultimately raising our children with the awareness of this gift, then the world will transform around us. Embrace your superpower.

"The great gift of human beings is that we have the power of empathy."
~ Meryl Streep

"God has never spoken to me directly, but I have heard him clear his throat."
~ Meister Eckhart

THE BODY

The body is the temple of the soul; we have just forgotten we are guests. Dr. Candace Pert has a great audio book called *The Body is the Subconscious Mind*, which describes my personal experience, as well. I believe that our subconscious mind is really just cellular memory, some from this lifetime, and some passed down genetically. The body is its own system with a profound intelligence, we've just forgotten how to communicate with our bodies, instead opting to own and dominate them.

Most of us agree that we aren't just physical beings, believing in an eternal energy or soul. If viewed in the polarity of masculine and feminine energy, the soul is masculine and the body is feminine, the two polarities combining to make a 3rd dimensional human. As with all things feminine, humans have spent thousands of years trying to eradicate this side of ourselves, loathing our mortal existence. I get it. I get homesick, too, but this method isn't helping, and it's starting to shift. More people are starting to care for our Earth and their bodies. They are just reflections of each other.

From the ancient ascetic religious practices to the obesity and drug addictions of today, we can easily see how we collectively feel about our physical existence, our feminine side. I know several people who think their bodies are amusement parks, here to enjoy without any consideration for physical wellbeing. Others demand a certain level of action from their bodies, like living on caffeine or working out constantly, even while their bodies are begging for a break. But what if we start to consider we are in partnership with a physical being? What if "our" body doesn't belong to us, it is just being a host to our consciousness? Would you be a better guest?

What does this have to do with intuition? Everything. The body has its own intelligence and receives way more information than we can gather with our conscious minds, the challenge is in understanding and using it. Well, the first challenge is awareness; just knowing it's there. The easiest way to begin is to establish a relationship with your body as a separate being, one you respect as a partner.

You know all those articles telling you what you should and shouldn't eat, drink, and do? In my experience, that whole thing never ends well. You spend a short time on some regimen, you can't stay on it (because it's just another way to force your will onto your body), you fall into self-loathing, and end up disliking your body even more. No need to "should" all over yourself. It's easier to come at it like a new friendship, with curiosity and lightness. Go ahead and have that cup of coffee, that glass of wine, and be open to how your body responds. Try not to judge it, just be aware of the subtle cues your body gives you, and respond appropriately. My body really reacts poorly to alcohol, and I am not right for days even after a single drink. I could be all upset that I "shouldn't" drink, but instead I happily choose to avoid alcohol because it's hard on my friend, my body.

As your friendship with your body deepens you will begin to pick-up on many more subtle cues. Your body will give you information about not just your energy, but on others around you. This is where your intuition can really come through. Once you really know your body, and how it communicates, you'll be surprised at all it can tell you.

EGO

Such a misunderstood creature, the ego. So many teachings telling us to suppress it, or conquer it, or otherwise annihilate it, when it's really a very useful thing to have while you're being human. Your ego is not the bad guy, but believing you are your ego is a dangerous business.

Your skin serves as a bag for your body, and an interface to the physical world. It's nice to have skin, but you know it's temporary; when your body dies, your skin goes with it. Your ego serves as a bag for your psyche, your emotions and thoughts, and as an interface with other people (or at least other people's egos). The ego is also temporary and dies with the body. The problem we're having is that we tend to believe we are our thoughts and emotions, instead of the more accurate description that we are experiencing thoughts and emotions. Our ego is just the lens we experience the world through, it is adaptable and changeable, and quite temporary.

Your ego is a valuable tool, once you realize it isn't who you are. You can work with it, and change it to suit your goals. Never treat it as the enemy, because it is an intrinsic part of being human, and it's a fabulous thing to have while you're here. Psychologically, losing your ego would be akin to physically losing your skin. You can live through it, but it sure makes it hard to function in this world. It's just better to form a partnership.

The ego is responsible for building the stories we collectively call our life. When we come across something new, the ego always tries to fit it into a pre-existing storyline. Here's where we hit a snag – the new information may have nothing to do with the old story, but the ego will find a way to make it fit. For example, a friend doesn't call when they said they would. If your existing storyline is into martyr-dom and self-pity, your brain automatically goes into "this always happens to me", judging and projecting and wallow-ing, when in reality, your friend had some kind of minor emergency and simply forgot. Human drama ensues.

The most effective way to work with the ego is de-tachment, and that is accomplished through awareness. Instead of being consumed by your reactions, step outside yourself and observe. When you start down that same old road of self-pity, mentally step back, and just be aware you are watching your ego at work. "Oh look, there's the mar-tyr script again." *Once you can disengage from being the story, then you can start creating a new story.* "I hope everything is okay with my friend. I'll send a text and go on with my day."

Is this an easy process? Nope, especially not in the beginning, but it gets easier over time. For an extra helping hand there are several effective techniques to accelerate the process, like EMDR, PSYCH-K, EFT, and others, but noth-ing takes the place of awareness. Only you can create a new version of yourself, and you must be present to do so.

So if you aren't your thoughts and emotions, who are you? You are the observer, the part of you that can watch your life without being consumed by it. Everyone is part hu-man and part Divine, part ego and part Spirit, and it is an ever-fluctuating mixture. When the ego takes up too much room, then we feel the lack of Spirit, resulting in all kinds of misery and mis-creation. The ego isn't inherently bad, we've just given it way more power than is healthy. *You are **not** your stories.*

Understanding and recognizing the ego is essential to developing your intuition. As information arrives intuitive-ly, the untrained ego will automatically try to bend it to be consistent with your current stories, even if it is totally unrelated. The image that comes to mind is the crotchety old woman reading tarot cards, and always predicting doom and gloom, not because it's there, but because it fits her own worldview. You need to know your own ego filters to minimize contamination of your intuition. We talk ourselves out of following our intuition daily because of the authority we give our ego's stories.

Awareness is the beginning of detachment. Be aware of your thoughts. Play with interrupting thought patterns that no longer serve. Start to identify as the observer. And above all else, know that you *aren't* your stories.

"The ego is not master in its own house."
~ Sigmund Freud

"Fear, to a great extent, is born of a story we tell ourselves, and so I choose to tell myself a different story."
~ Cheryl Strayed

THOUGHTS AND EMOTIONS

"I think, therefore I am" should be replaced with "I am, even though I think too much."

Thoughts and emotions are inexorably intertwined. We can create an emotional response with our thoughts, and when we experience an emotion, we find thoughts to justify it. The thing you can do to get back in the driver's seat is to be aware of your thoughts, change them when you need to, and be picky about what you feed your brain. These steps will ease the emotions as well, and allow you to be more receptive to your intuition. If you throw a rock into a turbulent river there's hardly a discernible effect, but throw a pebble into a still pond and you can't miss it.

Awareness is always the first, and most important, step. Know thyself. If you spend your day reacting to your environment (people, information), then you are operating on autopilot, you aren't really present. I'm not saying that being present and aware will negate all reactiveness, simply that the space between experiencing a reaction and acting on it is a choice point. There are lots of things in the world that make me feel angry or scared, but I get to choose how to respond, I have a still point after the feeling.

People tend to consider their thoughts to be some-how independent of them, and also more powerful. You are not a slave to your thoughts. The mind is a fabulous tool, but it works for you, not the other way around. You can interrupt a thought stream at any point, and redirect it to a calmer place. For example, when I was negotiating our union contract it was a contentious situation. Even on my peaceful drive home and on days off I would mentally argue my points. It got ridiculous. I decided that every time I found myself having this mental conflict, I would change the channel to peace signs and butterflies. I did this many times each day, and eventually my default thoughts were peaceful. Not always easy, but it can be done.

You are what you eat, even mentally. What you watch on television, the music you listen to, and the books and articles you read all make a huge difference to the quality of your thoughts. There is no wrong or right here, just be aware that different input changes your thought process and emotional state. Watching the news in video form, with the voice inflections, body language, facial expressions, and dramatic music is a very different experience than reading the news in print. Try switching to the other form for a week, and see if you notice a difference. What entertainment do you seek? Do you love watching dramas, but then complain your life is too dramatic? Hmm. Watch what you feed your mind.

When you are aware of your own thoughts and emotions, you become aware of other input entering your field, your intuition. The "still, small voice" is easily drowned out in the chaos of our thoughts and emotions. Seek to become the observer, to rise above the din. Still think, still feel, but find the still point between feeling and reaction. In this stillness lies the key.

"Let us not look back in anger, nor forward in fear, but around in awareness."
~ James Thurb

49

OBSERVING THE WORLD

CHAPTER 3

~ MEMORIES ~

I have always been an observer, never feeling quite human. From my earliest memories, I was always trying to figure out what makes people do the things they do. I still spend most of my time in a constant state of amazement.

When I was barely able to sit up on my own, I remember sitting on the kitchen floor playing with blocks and listening to my family discuss their beliefs. My Mom was a New Age hippie, Grandma was a devout Jehovah's Witness, and Grandpa was an Atheist. Very different philosophies, and each person was convinced they were right. As I sat and listened, I distinctly remember having my own dialog with one of my Guides: *Fascinating! They all think they are right, but none of them are. What makes people act this way?* My Guide didn't divulge any secret knowledge, he just talked with me as I tried to analyze the situation.

When I was just a toddler we went to clear out a recently deceased relative's house. There was a barking dog in the neighbor's fenced yard, and Grandma wasn't very happy that Mom wasn't carrying me. "The baby! You need to pick up the baby to keep her safe!" I could hear that she wasn't really concerned, that she knew I was fine, but she still put all this energy into objecting to my being allowed to walk on my own. *That's odd, I thought, why would she waste her energy declaring something she knows isn't true?* Several years later Mom was talking with a friend about when kids start retaining memories, and I shared this one. She recalled the situation, but was shocked that I did also.

I was playing in the dirt, digging holes behind the house when I had my first past-life memory. I was 3-years-old. Something in the moist soil smelled of death, and that smell threw me into a memory of falling into a pit of bodies, not quite dead myself. I remembered the cold of their dead skin, and the smell, and then rising out of my body. *That was awful! I don't want to do that again!* When the memory faded, I decided to go play somewhere else. The holocaust wasn't any more fun in hindsight.

I'm smart, but I'm even more competitive. My cousin, Tim, who is 2 months younger, started reading when we were three. After a couple weeks of hearing about how amazing he was, I couldn't take it anymore, and decided I needed to read, too. It took me half an hour to get through Hop on Pop, with my Mom telling me I didn't have to force it, but I made it all the way through. It was hard. When Tim started writing his own books a few months later, I let him have that one.

The first day of Kindergarten was my first real exposure to a group of kids my age. I really only knew my cousins before that. I remember thinking *I'm supposed to be one of these things, huh? They're really loud and they smell funny.* It took me several days to figure out why the teacher was telling us you could understand a story by looking at the pictures. Why wouldn't you just read the words? Oh, they can't read... right. School was my personal hell for the years I managed to stick with it.

It was around that time that my Grandma was talking about the calm, loving Jesus. Things like Prince of Peace and Lamb of God, meek and loving. I thought to myself *that isn't anything like the Jesus I knew. Maybe she's talking about a different Jesus.* The guy I knew was quite the rabble-rouser.

"Everybody needs his memories. They keep the wolf of insignificance from the door."
~ Saul Bellow

LAW OF ATTRACTION

It's funny to see how deep truths can be distorted by the human mind. It's also sad that so many suffer needlessly at the hand of distorted truth. But then again, we pay the ego to maintain our story, at any cost, even the cost of a lost Mystery.

The Law of Attraction is simply about vibrations attracting like vibrations. Unfortunately, it is currently used as a spiritually justified way to blame the victim, a normal trick of the ego. No one wants to feel vulnerable, so it is common to blame the victim for his or her own suffering. Think about how we discuss rape: she was drinking too much, she was alone, she was flirting, etc., so we can protect ourselves from feeling vulnerable: it won't happen to me, because I don't do those things. We also see it with cancer and other serious illness: he doesn't eat the right things, he doesn't take care of himself, he's so negative all the time so of course he's sick. Again, we mentally distance ourselves from the terrifying idea that it could just as easily happen to us.

There are several reasons why the Law of Attraction simply can't apply to every circumstance, but the biggest ego-hook to this half-truth is arrogance. You don't live in a bubble, and it isn't all about you. The original teaching was meant to promote empowerment, but has been derailed by a toxic mixture of control issues, blame, and denial. Instead of empowering our choices to help us make the most of our circumstances, it is now nothing more than a tool for judgment, of others and ourselves.

As with all misguided teachings, there is some truth in the mix. Your vibration most certainly matters, and attracts like vibrations, but it doesn't offer ultimate control over the tides of life. It allows us to rise or fall within each situation, which really is a lot of power and control, so attention needs to be paid to your thoughts and actions. But thinking you are personally responsible for every single thing around you rather misses the point. The teaching went from "when life gives you lemons, make lemonade" to "the lemons are all your fault, and if you could be a better person, you would only have strawberry daiquiris."

We are currently broadening our focus to include other beings. This is becoming more apparent as we enter the Age of Aquarius, and the collective takes a new position in our minds. The chemicals we dump in the water change the hormonal balance of every living creature that consumes it. And air pollution produced by a single industry touches lives all over the globe. An old system based on power and greed creates poverty and injustice. I don't care how high your personal vibration is, this is a collective effect.

And beyond the free will utilized by the collective, there has to be room for at least some version of Grand Design. No, I'm not excusing bad choices by playing the fate card; I'm simply saying creation involves other levels beyond human will. It's a co-creative process, and we need to allow room for the Mystery to happen.

Being fully empowered has more to do with reaction than creation. Life is about rising up to meet your circumstances, not being an infallible creator. I understand how we got here. There is a fine line between empowerment and control, and also between surrender and submission. I think the key is best stated in the Bhagavad Gita, when it tells us we may own our labor, but not the fruits of our labor. Both good and bad, you had a hand in it, just not the only hand.

The true tragedy of this misinterpretation is that it

limits the Law's effectiveness. The highest vibration you can reach is unconditional love, but issues of control and judgment naturally block this. Ironic, really. So let's change our focus to empowerment and radical self-love, and just sit in awe of the changes in the world around us.

"Self-love seems so often unrequited."
~ Anthony Powell

"Find a place inside where there's joy,
and the joy will burn out the pain."
~ Joseph Campbell

SPIRAL OF SPIRITUAL DEVELOPMENT

We would love our development to follow a linear progression, or maybe a stair-step, predictable series, but it simply doesn't work that way. I like the analogy of an upward spiral, where we continually see the same issues, but from a higher perspective, offering new and different insights. It is a life-long process, so we can never plan on reaching a final level where everything is always smooth. Life is never still; it is always either in growth or decay.

At the base of this spiral, we find conditioning: People living solely by virtue of social norm and expectations, without any contemplation of a bigger reality.

As we begin to rise, there is contemplation without action. This is where you find people beginning to question what they have been taught, but not changing anything. Here is where people think everything is ruled by fate or chance, thus relinquishing any power of free will.

At the next turn, free will dominates. People see the injustice around them, and are spurred into action (usually fueled by anger). This is where much of the world is today (2016). There is much societal change here, as people begin to find their power. At this point, free will is not only A thing, it's THE thing. Spiritually, it is where people jump into "law of attraction" type beliefs, where you are solely responsible for everything that presents itself in your life. This is where we develop our personal power, and our personal integrity.

Next up is the realization that you don't live in a bubble, nor is it all about you and your desires. Only after you reach a place of complete integrity and ownership of your personal power, can you look around and see the bigger picture. There are other people here, making choices that affect your life, and the world around you. Also, you hold DNA that may have been altered generations ago by a choice made by an ancestor. Not even your body is solely your own, regardless of your personal choices. Focus shifts from the individual to the collective (both past and present).

The next turn brings awareness of the non-physical world. While angels, demons, and aliens would have been only a superstition earlier in our growth, this new perspective shows us we are not alone. Without the firm foundation of personal power, this new information would throw us into fear or blame. Staying on the natural, spiral progression, we can assimilate this new information as simply new information. Energies completely outside our physical reality affect us, and we affect them. It is a totally different notion of personal responsibility. What we create matters on a much larger scale. Focus shifts from the physical reality to inter-dimensional awareness.

Next, we have an awareness of the macrocosm and the microcosm in perfect synchronicity, and the clear understanding of the sacred geometries holding them together. This is a very high mental realm, usually accessed through meditation (at least at first), and requires the upmost personal integrity to access in any meaningful or interactive way. This limited access is really for our safety, as someone who is still living in the "create your own reality" mode, wouldn't be the best person to be playing with the structure of the universe.

Lastly (on this first range of the spiral), we have connection with all; the I AM, completely devoid of personal ambitions.

And the spiral continues...

I know this is written in more of a step-by-step progression, but it is experienced much more fluidly. You may not even be able to mark the time when your beliefs begin to shift, and there is usually some ambiguity, or even regression, as you ascend. All this is normal. My point is simply to *let yourself evolve*. Do not cling to ideas once they no longer serve you. Learn, grow, experience, but keep moving. Also, it is important to fully experience each turn, and avoid "spiritual by-passing" at all costs. Just because you may be able to understand these progressions mentally, doesn't mean you have fully experienced them. You MUST go through the work of being fully empowered BEFORE you can move on. This is essential. If ANYTHING is still someone else's fault, then you still have work to do there.

Please be gentle with yourself and others. Please don't judge someone for being at a different level. You can't understand a level until you've experienced it. Likewise, you can't make someone progress. You can only hold the space of love and acceptance for others, while staying fully focused on yourself. And always keep climbing.

"Personal transformation can and does have global effects. As we go, so goes the world, for the world is us. The revolution that will save the world is ultimately a personal one."
~ *Marianne Williamson*

EMOTION & ATTACHMENT

Emotions have become much more complicated than they were originally designed to be. What we experience as emotion is only a chemical reaction in the physical body. Emotions are meant to make us feel, get our attention to notice what triggered them, and be released. Just a teaching tool, nothing more. They help us discern "good" experiences from "bad", and pleasure from danger. They assist in survival, as well as personal spiritual evolution.

The ego's job is to create stories; that's why we have one. We need an ego to maintain the illusion of duality, separation from Source and each other. The problem is, when we have an emotion, instead of just letting it be felt and leave the body, the ego attaches a story. From then on, the story triggers the emotion, and the emotion triggers the story. Biofeedback loop. That, my friends, is called a design flaw.

Then we add chemical addiction to the emotion itself, and we've really put ourselves in a hole. Now, we will subconsciously find a way to trigger the emotion, just to get a fix. At this point, no one is learning anything anymore, and can't figure out why they keep replaying the same story. What started as a chemically based teaching tool has taken on a life of its own. The emotional body and the pain body have both grown, if not originally formed, due to this biofeedback loop. In the original Mystery Teachings the four etheric bodies were physical, astral, mental, and spiritual. Only more recently do teachings refer to the emotional body instead of the astral body. Interesting, right?

Both the emotional body and the pain body are parts of the astral body. It is only through mental attachment to chemical emotions that we form and maintain these bodies. Or we inherited them. Yes, the chemicals of emotion, when not allowed to flow through and exit the body, actually change the DNA. So, whatever you don't clear is passed on to your offspring. Science has finally caught up on that one. I'm not saying emotions aren't real. They are very real. And the experiences that caused them are very real. But the story we attach to that emotional experience is subjective and fluid. For example, your Dad hit you at Christmas one year while he was drinking. The experience happened. You had an emotional reaction. However, how you view the incident changes with time. At first, maybe you were angry in general, then at men, then at alcohol, then a greater understanding of addiction, then it changes to compassion for your Dad's pain, etc. The story changes over time with your own experiences. The problem is the tighter you hold the story, the more attachment to recreating the emotion.

Never fear, there is a solution. It begins, you guessed it, with awareness. In order to clear these emotional charges they must be noticed (or remembered), fully felt, and the story released. The process is simple, but the work is messy. Most people want to remember the event, and go straight to releasing it. That's called "spiritual bypassing", and it never truly heals the wound.

I think we are all a little wary of fully feeling our emotions because on some level we recognize the little biofeedback loop issue. Understandable. No one wants to get lost in the astral body. But the feeling part is essential to clear the chemical from the physical body. It's almost like the emotional chemical lodges itself in the body, until it is felt and acknowledged, like its job isn't complete until it's felt. Once you fully feel it, it can leave, provided you don't have a mental attachment (story).

Try this process... identify an emotional event, release or rewrite the story, fully feel the emotion involved, thank it and release it. Fill any empty spaces with Divine Love, and let the healing begin. If you feel the emotion come up again in a similar way (same story), fully feel it, thank it, and release it, then become aware of patterns or lingering attachments. Be aware, and make changes, but release the emotion.

Emotions must be felt, but only as a passing wave. Don't allow the ego to build a story around every emotion. Awareness is the key.

"There are two kinds of people. One kind you can just tell by looking at them at what point they congealed into their final selves. It might be a very nice self, but you know you can expect no more surprises from it. The other kind keep moving forward and making new trysts with life, and the motion of it keeps them young. In my opinion, they are the only people who are still alive. You must be constantly on your guard against congealing."
~ Gail Godwin

FAITH, BELIEF, AND DOGMA

After literally a couple of decades pondering the true meaning of faith, I have finally made enough progress to share. Not that this is my final answer, but it's still worth consideration.

I have always been told that I have unshakable faith. I have also been at a loss here, because most of my beliefs are based in personal, direct experience, not accepting someone else's story. I have always said I don't have faith, I have direct experience. I considered the terms *faith* and *belief* to be interchangeable, being that they are both understood to refer to something other than direct experience. To say "I believe in something" or "I have faith in something" seemed like the same thing. The thing is, those words aren't interchangeable, after all.

Dogma is easier to define, if possibly harder to see in ourselves. Once a belief becomes solidified, it turns into dogma. How can you tell when this happens? Dogma is present when there is only one right way, and it applies to everyone. It is commonly associated with religion, but it is just as pervasive in science, politics, nationalism, and finance, to name a few. Dogma is the result of a mind closed by its beliefs, and unwilling to allow room for other options to even be heard, let alone examined.

We all know that extreme religious type, who is busy condemning others for not living up to their chosen standards, but look at other areas. Do you know someone who has so much pride in his or her country, that the rest of the entire globe is doing it wrong? What about that friend who defends everything science is currently professing, without the willingness to consider some of it may be outdated theory in only a few years? Western medicine? The military?

I've even seen some amazingly dogmatic beliefs within the New Age and spiritual communities. We currently live in a dogmatic culture, which encourages unquestioning obedience to whatever beliefs you hold. The only way to break the hold of dogma is to question everything.

Beliefs are a more fluid thing, and can still be influenced by new information and experiences. Beliefs form the box we live in, and we can change them out, or at least expand them, when we see fit. We all believe in something. Even if direct experience is our foundation, stories must be created to fill in the gaps, to create a safe space for our ego to wonder. The ego keeps the box of our beliefs in tact as best it can. That's what we pay it for. The illusion of separation requires the formation of the ego to keep the curtain up. Beliefs are essential, but changeable. By changing your beliefs, you change your experience of the world.

Faith is a whole different matter. Faith is a mystical experience, completely independent of belief systems. It is the subtle certainty that you are loved and safe, no matter what the outside world looks like, no matter what your current story. It's not "I have faith in God/dess" or "I have faith in Divine order." If your faith is in something, then it is really just a belief, no matter how strong a belief it is. Faith is simply "I have faith." It is the ability to surrender entirely to the Mystery, with complete trust that you are always safe. As with all mystical experiences, words are only a shadow of the meaning they try to convey.

Faith is the ability to truly live in the Mystery, if even for a few fleeting moments. Completely undefined, without the ego-comfort of belief. It is totally expansive. Of course, as soon as the ego catches a glimpse of this, terror ensues. Talking about living in the Mystery, and actually doing it, are very different things. But the ability to completely re-

lease definition, even for a moment, is Faith.
And yes, I have Faith.

*"Faith is taking the first step even when
you don't see the whole staircase."*
~ *Martin Luther King, Jr.*

*"Faith is the strength by which a shattered world
shall emerge into the light."*
~ *Helen Keller*

DEATH

Ever think about death? Ever think about when and why it became such a bad thing? One of my biggest pet peeves is when a death announcement includes the implication of failure: "she lost her battle with cancer" "after a long struggle, he succumbed to the disease" "she fought hard, but was finally overcome." What? Seems to me, if we came here to be mortal, then by dying we have succeeded in our journey. Good job on that mortality thing – you lived right up until you died!

Let's not confuse death with grief. Death is always hardest on the living because grieving is a painful process, and it happens regardless of your personal philosophical beliefs on a potential afterlife. It's hard to have a hole in your life where a loved one used to be. Healing takes time, and it's a process unto itself. But all of that despair is for the living, and is really about loss, not death.

I imagine death used to be considered part of the cycle of life, when we used to honor cycles. Once upon a time, we viewed time as both cyclical and linear, marking the change of the seasons, and marking our age in reference to how many cycles we'd seen. Then we changed our focus to an almost entirely linear concept of time, with a beginning and an end, instead of a constant circle. This change is a reflection of our collective misogyny by ignoring the cyclical (feminine) nature of time in favor of a linear (masculine) view. Our loss. Now we are in a constant race to an inevitable end point that everyone fears.

Why do we fear death, when it's really only hard on the living? Well, once the concept of judgment came onto the scene... and then there's hell... who makes this stuff up? Oh right, we do. In the extensive history of human beliefs, hell didn't show up until about 850 BCE, introduced by a guy named Zoroaster. It got muddled in with the Yahweh cult (Jewish religion), and then emphasized by Christianity, most likely because fear is a great crowd control. While many previous beliefs include some form of assessment or afterlife, they don't include condemnation or a cosmic battle of good and evil. Trust me, this is worth some research if you have fear of judgment after death.

On top of the religious issues, we have the medical industrial complex jumping on the bandwagon. It is implied, in all the recommended screening and treatments, that if you follow their (rather expensive) protocol, you can somehow elude aging and death. No, they never outright say that, but it is most definitely implied. If it weren't, people wouldn't go to the extremes of surgery and chemo. Think how much money would be lost if people no longer feared death. Let that sink in a bit. In my experience, people tend to live right up until they die, regardless of drastic medical intervention.

So let's sum it up, shall we? We came here to live a mortal life, to experience time, aging, and eventually death, as a completely natural and expected process, then we decided it was bad and scary to age and die, so we cling to youth and life in complete defiance of the reason we came here in the first place. Only humans could screw things up this bad.

The first step out of this mess is to reconsider life and death as a natural cycle. Figure out where you get scared and stuck and why. Fear? Conformity? Just haven't given it much thought? The only way to move forward on any topic is to bring your beliefs to light, to really be willing to dig out your own subconscious and decide what to release. Here's a hint: If you believe something only because that's what you were taught, it needs extra attention. If you didn't examine and choose a belief yourself, then you are running on autopilot.

After we have reconciled our beliefs on death (which could take years), then we can get to the good stuff... is it really necessary? Is death more of a habit, a cultural norm? Before you completely walk away from this discussion, consider that science is currently asking that same question, with some pretty amazing results. At this point (2015), science is flirting with the idea of "curing death" through gene manipulation. Saving the moral implications for another time, it may soon be possible to step out of the cycle of life and death. Science and technology are a reflection of human consciousness; we can watch them to see ourselves expand.

Play with it a bit, the idea of death. I've found starting at the end helps me to clear my head.

"The fear of death follows from the fear of life.
A man who lives fully is prepared to die at any time."
~ Mark Twain

69

SUBTLE ENERGY

CHAPTER 4

∾ Accidental Exorcism ∾

Although this is pretty funny in hindsight, don't try this at home. Exorcism is very real, and requires training for everyone's safety.

I had been sharing an emotional body with Steve, my second Twin Flame, for about nine months, and it had been a rough road. 42 was probably the hardest year of my life, and I was really looking forward to my birthday. Steve had fallen off my radar a few days earlier, as he did whenever he dropped into a depression. Maybe our frequencies no longer aligned, maybe the Gods were having mercy on me. The day before my birthday he made a public post about dying by his own hand. I lost it. I called Adriane, my Sister Twin Flame, crying like a baby.

"I didn't sign up for this! I can't handle a suicidal Twin! I feel like my heart is being ripped in half, and he doesn't even know we're connected!" Adriane talked me down, with all the skill and grace of the angel she is, then she said, "I got this. Don't worry about a thing, I'll talk to some people* and take care of it. You just go have your birthday. It'll be fine." (*people meaning the High Counsel in higher dimensions)

I felt it when Adriane started her work. She's a badass. The only problem was she was trying to completely separate Steve and I, which isn't even an option with Twins. It hurt. I wanted to puke and pass out. I thought *I need to call her and tell her to stop. That's possibly the stupidest thing I've ever thought. I'll just go to the Counsel myself.* And that's what I did. I heard them tell her she couldn't cut everything, but there were other options... the pain stopped and I left her to it.

The next morning I woke up and felt... nothing. It was glorious! I couldn't feel Steve, I couldn't feel Adriane, I couldn't even feel myself. Such blissful oblivion! Glorious solitude! I had a fabulous birthday. The next day I still felt nothing, which was fine, but I couldn't even check-in with Adriane, an ability we've had for years. I decided to utilize technology and give her a call. It wasn't good.

"I feel awful. Completely depressed and suicidal. The voices in my head keep telling me how worthless I am and I don't deserve to live. I can barely function."

I said, "Wait a minute. Steve always talks about his demon saying those things, but I think he thinks he's joking about the demon part. Did you do an exorcism?"

"Not on purpose!" she said. "I was cutting cords and things, and it seemed fine, then I woke up this way. I feel like I'm drowning. I'm too weak to fight it."

Well shit. Now what? So I said the only thing I could, "I got this. Don't worry about it, I'll talk to some people and take care of it. You just go to bed. It'll be fine."

Now, Adriane does this kind of work all the time, so whatever she was battling had to be pretty powerful. I closed my eyes, spun up my Merkabah, called in Archangel Michael, and disappeared into the 5th dimension. When I saw the demon in question, it stopped me in my tracks. I've never seen anything that big and ugly. It wasn't in Adriane, it was much bigger than that, and it was attached and feeding through her 3rd chakra. Well shit. I double-checked my armor, made sure I still had Archangel Michael by my side, checked my fear at the door, and into the fray I went.

It took longer than my previous experiences of expelling entities, and it left some significant damage. I called in Archangel Rafael to repair her energy body. I also set up a healing chamber around Steve, since I was sure there was damage there also. The demon was finally gone, but what a mess.

The next day Adriane was her old self, all happy and demon-free. Steve emailed me and just said, "I feel really funny. Are you doing something over there?"

"Well, there was sort of an accidental exorcism..."

"If it's the Psychic Network why do they need a phone number?"
~ Robin Williams

SUBTLE ENERGY

Energy encompasses everything in both physical and non-physical realms, including random thoughts and emotions. Physical reality is shaped first energetically, and then we experience it in the "real" world. We are each creating our reality with our thoughts and attention, whether we know it or not. Quantum physics is beginning to demonstrate our effect on subtle energy in a more scientific and socially acceptable way; it's no longer a matter of woo-woo alone.

Nikola Tesla had it right: "Think of the universe in terms of frequency and vibration." As we develop ways to measure and quantify subtle energy, we will start to understand how "reality" really works. For example, most of us have heard that love and gratitude are of a higher frequency, but instead of taking that as literal we tend to think that having a positive attitude is just more comfortable for others, so they want us to behave that way. This isn't about positive thinking as such; this is about our power to actually change the vibration of our very cells. Along this line, karma isn't a judgment / punitive system, it is simply a matter of attracting like vibrations. This is science, or at least where science is going.

Energy workers are simply people who have learned to navigate the world of subtle energy, and focus it in certain ways. Energy workers can use "unmarked" energy, as taught in Reiki or Quantum Touch, to assist in a situation. "Unmarked" simply means there is no intention, no agenda, attached. So, sending energy to a sick cat might result in recovery or death, depending on what the cat needs to do, because the energy is just there to assist in the highest good, not to bend reality to one's will. How could we be okay helping Fluffy die? What I wonder is how could others think they know better than God/Goddess when a life should end? Sending energy without an intention (even an intention to heal) is always safest, because fate takes care of itself.

Using energy with an intention requires a bit more skill. We do it all the time in our own lives, and this awareness can change your world. People like things to be black and white, fate OR free will, but it is always a combination of my will and Thy will. Directing energy in your own life is between you and the Divine. Using energy to assist a friend, with their consent, is supporting their free will choice. Sending energy to someone marked with an intention (even to heal), without their consent, is treading on both their free will and fate. This stuff is real. Before you direct an intention at someone, consider the implications. What is the harm in asking their permission? Or in just sending unmarked energy for the highest good?

There are also warnings about doing no harm (or black magic) because it will return to you. Again, this isn't a matter of morality (though it has moral significance), but of frequency. In order to send out lower vibrational energies you must build, or call, them through your own body, which causes your personal vibration to lower and attract similar energies. Much more can be attained by always working with the Light (higher frequencies).

To start working with your own energy, start with a simple breath meditation, followed by a mental gratitude list. Be very aware of the sensations in your body. Just like learning anything new, this will take practice, but everyone can do it. At first you may feel nothing at all, but just keep doing it for a few minutes each day, and pretty soon you will even feel a difference in just focusing on your breath. If you want more structured training, find a Quantum Touch class, or whatever you are drawn to. Once you start to experience your own energy, you'll look at the world in a whole new way.

"If you want to find the secrets of the universe, think in terms of energy, frequency and vibration."
~ Nikola Tesla

"The day science begins to study non-physical phenomena, it will make more progress in one decade than in all the previous centuries of its existence."
~ Nikola Tesla

ENTITIES AND EXORCISM

The topic of non-physical entities generally freaks people out. Either they spiral down into fear, or they think it's a crazy idea, or both. Let's try to find a different angle on the subject by starting with invisible, physical beings, like bacteria or intestinal parasites. You can't see them without special equipment, yet they are so real they can be life threatening. We simply haven't yet invented the equipment needed to locate and identify non-physical life forms. We will. Until then, we have people who can sense, work with, or remove these energies.

Along with knowing they exist, also know they come in many forms. Everything from angels and demons to parasitic energy suckers, to inter-dimensional beings. Some are helpful, some are just like mosquitoes (just survival feeding, not malicious), and some are down right nasty. It's just like the variety of creatures in our physical reality. In fact, think of the range of awareness just within the human species... we may all be conscious, but some are definitely more conscious than others.

Just like you take antibiotics to kill off harmful bacteria, and probiotics to encourage the growth of helpful bacteria, we can do something similar with non-physical entities. Building up the good ones happens through payer and meditation. Actively building a relationship with your Guides, Guardians, and Angels, and inviting their presence and assistance is essential. Others can guide you in various techniques, but the daily practice is up to you. Your relationship with your unseen support team is ultimately your responsibility.

Now for the unwanted energies... there are people who can assist in removal, but again, it is you who is ultimately responsible for keep them out. For example, some parasitic entities feed on fear and drama. You go to a professional to have these entities removed, but you continue to watch the news every night, and gossip endlessly. They'll be back. You are responsible for your own energy leaks. At this point, I'll only do entity removals for people who are dedicated to a path of spiritual growth. People wouldn't need as many antibiotics, if they would take responsibility for their health by taking care of themselves. Same thing, only entity removal can be quite a bit trickier than just taking a prescription. Can you do this on your own? Sometimes. By changing your lifestyle and raising your vibration, you simply aren't an emotional buffet anymore, and many will find somewhere else to go. For some of the heavier stuff (yes, demons exist), you will need to find assistance. NEVER attempt to remove an entity from someone else without training and guidance. It usually isn't a traumatic event if you know what you're doing, but protections need to be in place, and protocols followed, for everyone's safety. Just like a virus, you can't see it, but it's dangerous, all the same.

If you wish to explore this fairly uncharted territory, first dedicate yourself to a spiritual path, and get your own energy as clear as possible. Then find a good teacher to show you the ropes. Yes, there are tons of videos on Shamanism or the Merkabah, but nothing compares to an actual teacher. With a guide to help you avoid some of the common pitfalls, it's a beautiful, non-physical universe out there.

CHANNELING

Channeling is a word that begs definition, but is hard to pin down. It's like saying you're Christian, which encompasses hundreds of sects, everything from Unitarian to Evangelical to Catholic to Mormon, with the only common thread being some kind of acceptance of Jesus as the Messiah and Yahweh as God. The term is just too broad. Same thing with channeling. Some people speak in tongues, and others just feel guided to say certain things in conversation, and there is a whole range in between. The common ground for the word is simply that information comes through you, not from you We all channel to some extent, or at least we all have the ability, some are just more aware of the process.

I am often asked how I know that I'm only channeling something "good" and not something "evil." It is so sad to me that we have developed such a fear of the unseen, and such a polarity and conflict of good vs. evil. First of all, the energetic world isn't divided into only angels and demons, and no one is trying to capture your soul. Just let that whole story go, and come at this from a more rational perspective. Seriously. Think of it like strep or staph – everyone carries these microbes on their skin all the time, invisible and innocuous, and they only cause illness when the immune system is out of balance. Strep and staph aren't inherently evil, they are just part of our world. Yes, we are surrounded by unseen energies (some advanced enough to be called entities) all the time, but they're just hanging out doing their thing, not looking for ways to ruin our lives.

Much of it comes down to personal vibration. If you have a higher vibration, then you will attract other beings (in this world and the next) with a similar vibration. If you spend most of your time in fear or anger, then you will attract beings that resonate with you. Some of these energies are parasitic, and actually feed on the energy of lower emotions. Don't dwell on negative feelings or you're going to feel drained from being the buffet. Again, this is just the way these things work, they aren't out to get you, and changing your vibration means they will no longer resonate with you and will just wonder off. Not a big deal.

When anyone channels anything, the goal is to step out of the way (move the ego over) to allow information to flow through you, but no matter how "clear" a channel is, the information is always colored by that person's personality. Keep this in mind when you receive channeled information, or start to channel on your own. I knew a woman who channeled Mother Mary, and her messages always fluctuated wildly between the love of Mary and the fear of this woman's ego. It was obvious when she was getting in the way. Anything fear-based is from a lower vibration, either a lower entity or your own ego. Same with power (over others), vengeance, pride (I'm more special than you), and greed (lack).

I'm not saying you'll never get "bad" news from a channeled source, only that it won't be intended in a way that encourages drama. You might be told that the career you want isn't part of the plan, but it will be only that, not all the baggage we create around why we didn't get what we wanted (I'm not worthy, god hates me, I'm a bad person). Judgment is a human thing; we make up reasons when it's really just the path we came to walk.
Many people start channeling using spontaneous writing – either in a journal or typing. I started with the spoken word, as a counselor. How do I know when I'm channeling and when I'm just talking? I have been doing it so long I can feel my energy shift, but at first it was only after the fact

that I knew. The less your ego is involved, the less memory you have of the event. After a counseling session I could remember the basic topics, but not the specific words. I've had many people say a certain conversation helped them immensely, and I have little or no recollection of it, not because it didn't matter to me, but because it came through me not from me.

"People hear that and say I'm being modest,
but I am not a modest person,
but I have to be truthful about what
I'm doing and what I'm doing is channeling."
~ Morgan Freeman

MANIFESTATION

Everything you've been taught about manifesting is wrong. Let's just start there. Actually, the common teachings work quite well, but always include unintended side effects. For example, calling for rain, in a drought, in the middle of August, with no precipitation forecast, and having it rain for three days... and flood the basement. Really happened to me. I couldn't make this stuff up.

In case you don't know, the popular teachings show how to manifest with the mind, using focused will (3rd chakra). You focus on what you want, add emotion, release it to the Universe, and miracles happen. And they do. But manhandling fate just never ends well. This is where we get the fear of magic, and the notion that magic always comes at a price.

I have played with various concepts of manifestation for several years, a lot of trial and error. I had reached the conclusion that manifesting by will alone wasn't the way to go, when I took an online class by Drunvalo Melchizedek, and he explained it so simply. He said that the brain has two hemispheres and is limited to logic, so creating with the mind always has two opposite results, and taking more at one end will create lack somewhere else. It's best to manifest through the heart.

Why isn't it always taught this way? Because working through the mind gives the ego (our personal desires) full control, and we get to feel really powerful when we bend the world to our will. Working through the heart is about co-creation with the divine, and requires a lot of letting go, something humans kinda suck at. When manifesting with the heart, you leave most of the details out, and trust the Universe to bring exactly what you need. Trust is also an issue for most, even trusting God/Goddess.

It's a good idea to work with the heart regularly, so it's in shape for the work of manifesting. How? Gratitude is the gateway drug to manifesting with the heart. Every night before you fall asleep, list (either mentally or in a journal) 3 things you're grateful for. Start simple: I am so grateful for the food I ate today, my cat, the sound of the rain. When this list making becomes habit, start practicing gratitude at the time of the event. Instead of enjoying being in the warm sun, truly feel grateful. Yes, there's a difference.

The next step is letting go of complete control and increasing trust in the Divine. This is mostly a matter of mindfulness. As you go about your daily life, notice when you feel frustrated and impatient, and ask yourself why. Why am I attached to a certain outcome? If all things have Divine timing, why am I in a hurry? Why do I feel like I know better than the Universe when and how things should work out? It's a humbling process, I can assure you, but so worth it.

The more adept you become with opening your heart, and letting go and trusting the Universe, the easier and faster the creation process becomes. Promise.

Finally the good stuff... it really is pretty simple. Let's call on rain the right way.

Visualize the outcome – a green lawn after a rain.

Feel the outcome – (emotionally) I am so happy and relieved that it rained.

Release it to the Universe – I give it to God/Goddess, and *release all attachment to the result.* I trust that what needs to happen will happen.

Gratitude – I am grateful for the support of the Universe, and its help in the co-creation process. I trust that the outcome will be perfect.

Gratitude – (emotionally) I go through a mental gratitude list, both to activate the heart, and to pull my mind away from the task at hand. It helps the process of letting go.

Manifesting with the heart is a process of release and surrender. If you notice you are really focusing (especially on the details of the outcome), then you've slipped into using the will. Our whole society promotes living though the will, so don't be surprised if you go there. Living through the heart takes practice, and it is truly a dance with the Divine.

"The dancer's body is simply the luminous manifestation of the soul."
~ Isadora Duncan

"All life is a manifestation of the spirit, the manifestation of love."
~ Morihei Ueshiba

NEW MANIFESTATION

Magnetizing is the new manifesting. We are currently (2015) redefining creation, and all the old manifesting rules are out the window. At least for some of us, and that number will grow to encompass most of us by 2020. When the old way of manifesting stops working for you, when everything driven by personal will seems to fall apart, you'll know it's time to magnetize.

Magnetizing is simply drawing in experiences (people, opportunities, stuff) with your energy field. There is little room for personal will (or ego), because strengthening your energy field requires you to simply be more you. Get closer to the true vibration of your unique soul. So the only place for personal willpower is to commit to doing those things that increase your being. Whatever it is that connects you to your bliss, do more of that. No, I'm not saying quit your job, I'm saying make your soul a priority and new job opportunities may pop up. All kinds of unexpected things start appearing as you move into magnetizing your world.

This isn't a new concept; "follow your bliss" has been taught throughout the ages. It was always ONE way, but now it's THE way. For good reason, things will now only manifest if they are aligned with our soul vibration. All of the chaos and tragedy in the world today is a product of manifesting by willpower alone, driven by the dark recesses of the ego, greed and power. The soul vibration has no use for power and greed, so its creations will look completely different. The only thing that will make this transition difficult is our attachments, our ego.

Everyone wants to feel in charge of their life, to make things happen. Empowerment is a big deal, and we are being asked to be empowered as we surrender to our own

Higher Self. Let's not confuse surrender with inaction. This is still a co-creative process, and we are each *required* to be fully present and aware, and to act on our inner guidance, but now we are required to follow that guidance instead of ignoring it. If you want things to keep moving in your life, you have to move toward your soul. No more demanding things happen a certain way, just because you said. The collective energy no longer supports it.

This is going to be a bit of a shock to those who think they are following their hearts, only to find the ego has been running the show. For example, let's use a massage therapist. Someone might say to themselves *I love being a massage therapist! I'm helping people. So why is my business falling apart now?* Well, if "helping people" really meant fulfilling an ego need to be a martyr or a savior, and the energy is no longer supporting ego endeavors, then they will simply stop attracting clients. Does this mean they need to change careers? Possibly. Or at least understand, and release, the ego attachment to the work. Awareness and release are pure magic, all by themselves.

Along with releasing ego gratifications, we are also releasing fear, by increasing trust in our own Higher Selves. The sense of duality and separation has been so strong in this world, many of us don't really trust in the Divine. We say we believe in a Higher Power, but at the same time we feel like this life is totally up to us and no one really has our back. This underlying fear is why we have so many issues around control, and feeling like we have to make things happen, instead of *allowing* things to happen. I can tell you that the Universe fully supports you, and it does, but the only way to know it is to start building a personal relationship with the unseen. They're eagerly awaiting your attention.

So how do you strengthen your soul vibration to magnetize all the good stuff? It's different for everyone. Start by doing whatever empties your mind and brings you fully into the present moment – that may be yoga, gardening, singing, painting, running, baking, whatever. You know what brings you to that place of inner stillness. After each session with your soul, take a minute to really feel the gratitude for this time of connection. Do this daily, even for 20 minutes, and the world will start to change.

This is where you get to (have to) use your personal willpower... commit to yourself and this process. You can make 20 minutes to spend with your soul everyday if you simply decide it's a priority, and it will become a priority for everyone soon. The sooner you align your personal will with the vibration of your soul, the easier the next few years will be. This is what surrender is – aligning your will with Higher Will. This is why surrender is an active, not passive, process. Align and thrive. I'm telling you, it's amazing.

As you continue with this process, your intuition grows, and the more you follow it, the more it grows. It's a spiral. You put more soul vibration into the world, the Universe responds by supporting that effort, in amazing and unexpected ways. You become a magnetic field, naturally drawing in what you need. Your only job is to be more you, and the Universe will supply the rest.

"Magnetism, as you recall from physics class, is a powerful force that causes certain items to be attracted to refrigerators."
~ Dave Barry

MYSTERY SCHOOL

CHAPTER 5

~ Surfing the Void ~

My mission has always been to assist in raising the collective consciousness of humanity. I felt my mission end in October 2008. I thought *that's weird. If the mission is over, why am I still here?* Like I would suddenly blink out of existence, or something. A few days later my body started shutting down – I was dying. Nothing gets your attention faster than major organs failing, that's for sure.

At this point, the anger surged, knowing that I put in all this work and wasn't going to see the dawn of the New Age in 2012. The mission was successful, but no one asked if I was ready to go. I went into meditation and stormed into the library where the Akashic Records are kept, demanded to rewrite mine, and basically threw a fit like a two-year-old. Turns out they won't help you unless you act like an adult. I cooled down for a couple days, went back, and re-wrote my contract the right way. Two weeks later, I fell into the void.

Flashback 18 years to 1990... After my Grandma died, my Mom appeared to have a psychotic break followed by sever depression. She just wasn't the same. When I would ask her about it, she would say, "I lost my ego." I thought that was the most ridiculous thing I'd ever heard. People don't just lose their ego! Enlightenment is a myth, and she didn't seem happy at all. Now I get it.

Right before I fell in, I was trying to work out why education doesn't always expand people's minds. I would like to think religious extremes could be avoided if only everyone had access to information. But then I kept going back to the Mormons – upper middle class, access to information, and they still believe it's their duty to baptize by proxy. Really? Why?

The last visual I had was like I was tugging at loose strings on a tapestry, and then I realized it wasn't lack of education, it was belief systems created by the ego. As soon as I thought that the whole tapestry fell apart, and I thought *shit... I'm never getting that put back together.* Then it was just dark and silent... for the next sixteen months.

Growing up an Indigo, I always had open dialog with my guides, visions, and all kinds of extrasensory stuff going on, so when it all quit it was the first time I'd been really alone. Dark and quiet. What can you say about nothing? No chattering mind rambling off grocery lists, no colorful visions of the future, no connection to anyone or anything. No way to get back to the Akashic Records to change my mind. Dark and silent.

A few weeks into this, my Mom asked what was wrong, because I seemed so different. I explained what had happened, and she replied, "Told you I lost my ego." I apologized profusely, but she wasn't upset. She said it couldn't be explained, only experienced. That's an understatement. I asked her how long it took for her voices to come back, and she said they hadn't. She was afraid to let them start again for fear she couldn't stop them.

Screw that. I wanted my ego back. I missed me, and all my invisible friends. I'm not sure if enlightenment is different from ego death, but the latter is more descriptive of the process I went through. Liberating, I'll give you. Once you see that everything is a story and you lose all attachment, you are under no obligation to believe anyone's bullshit, even your own. I did my best to encourage the regrowth of my ego, but every time I would get the monkey mind to start up, I would think *yeah, but it's all made-up,* and it would go quiet again.

I learned a couple interesting things during my months in the void. Emotions are primarily a chemical reaction, thus being a physical phenomenon. I would still feel angry or sad, but without the ability to attach a story, the chemicals would run through my system like a quick wave. I couldn't dwell, because it requires attachment to a story. I also learned that all guided meditation and energy work require the imagination, which is a function of the ego. Without the ego it's just dark and quiet. Really, really, dark and quiet.

When I try to explain the experience people usually say, "That happened to me once! One time after yoga my mind went totally quiet for like 20 minutes!" Yeah, that's cute. Sixteen months is a lot of silence. It's been over six years now, and there are still big holes where I used to be. Ego: you sure will miss it when it's gone.

My Mom died unexpectedly in March 2010. The only good thing about it was that I could feel some attachment to her and our story together. I thought well, *at least maybe*

I'll finally get my ego back. Now I refer to this time as the "post-void apocalypse" because after you get liberated, then your shadow gets liberated. It's really the most horrible thing I've ever been through. The ego was there, but it wasn't integrated with me as the observer. It was more like suddenly sprouting a semi-formed conjoined twin, who is prone to tantrums. It just wasn't pretty. That part lasted another year and a half, or so.

Since then, integration has been slow, but improving. I got my invisible friends and my ability to meditate back just before the apocalypse phase. I still really miss the passion for life. I used to be able to get all wound up about things that upset me, or be really driven by my goals. I can't quite get there anymore, at least not for any length of time. Part of me always says *yeah, but it's all made up...* and it really is.

"Enlightenment is a destructive process.
It has nothing to do with becoming better or
being happier. Enlightenment is the crumbling
away of untruth. It's seeing through the facade
of pretense. It's the complete eradication
of everything we imagined to be true."
~ Adyashanti

MYSTERY SCHOOL TEACHINGS

As I sit down to explain what Mystery School teachings are, I understand why there's so much mystery involved. It's a bit like trying to catch smoke in your hands. That's why there is so much symbolic language, and vague mystical direction involved. "The door to the sanctuary is within." "Know thyself." "Magic flows through an open heart." Lots of fingers pointing to the moon, but no practical guidance on where you're going or how to get there. Remember those mazes on the back of kid's menus? I always started at the end, so I wouldn't get lost. Cheating? If you think so, you'd best stop reading, because we're going to start at the end.

A Mystery School is a vibration, not a knowledge base. There are several Mystery Schools, each with their own story and dogma, but they all deliver you to the door within, to a higher vibrational way of existing.

Visualize a person standing with their arms out to the sides, looking like a cross. Nothing Christian here, it's just the shape of a human standing with their arms out. The right arm represents the mental body, the left arm represents the emotional (or astral) body, the legs and feet the physical, the crown of the head the spiritual connection. When we are on our mental crazy train or refusing to think (contemplate), we're experiencing life from the right hand fingertips. Emotional drama or disconnection, the left hand fingertips. Either loathing our body or using it as a carnival ride, our toes. Zoning out through meditation or even psychedelic drugs puts us up at the top of the head. So here's how our lives usually look:

Ugh! I don't want to go to work! My life sucks because... (right fingertips)

If I'm gonna do all this, I need to have more energy.

Coffee! Wheee, caffeine! (toes)

My day was stressful, I need a drink. (toes & left fin-gertips)

I have to call my friend and gossip! (left fingertips)
The weekend – time to party! (toes and possibly both sides of fingertips)

I need a yoga retreat to get me back on track (head)
I still hate my life because... (fingertips)

And on, and on, and on...

See how we bounce around the edges, making a dia-mond shape between toes, fingertips and head? We nor-mally live on the superficial edges of life, never making it to the center.

The Mystery Schools are about the center, living from the heart. In the center (heart) all is in balance. The heart is not mental, but it receives intuition. The heart is not emo-tional, but it pours out unconditional love. The heart is not only physical or spiritual, but where divinity meets matter, and the spark of Life is safely held in the body of Creation.

And that's where you find the door.

In the past, a person would spend decades or a whole lifetime deciphering mystical meanderings just to get to this basic understanding. The energy now supports a much faster progression, and these words will resonate with many. Not to worry, no Mystery School teachings have been violated by sharing these insights; knowing where to look, and being able to do so are very different things. Knowing the destination just gives you a sense of direction, but getting there takes more diligence and dedi-cation than most are willing to put forth. You must walk the path yourself, under the basic guidance of all Hermetic teachings: Know Thyself.

"Let my soul smile through my heart
and my heart smile through my eyes,
that I may scatter rich smiles in sad hearts."
~ Paramahansa Yogananda

"The best and most beautiful things in
the world cannot be seen or even touched -
they must be felt with the heart."
~ Helen Keller

KNOW THYSELF

At first glance, most people think they know themselves quite well; after all, they've lived with themselves all their lives. We know our favorite color and our religion and what foods we prefer, but there are two things most people don't know: why am I the way I am, and who was I born to be? These are the questions the Mystery Schools demand we ask, and keep asking our entire lives. It is a never-ending process, because as we change and grow, so do the answers.

Start with looking at every avenue of your life and ask *why?* I love football... *why?* I dislike cats... *why?* I am patriotic... *why?* I am religious... *why?* As you go through the layers, it will usually end up with "that's what I was taught." And this is why the unexamined life is not worth living. If you are just running on conditioning then you aren't really you at all, just a shadow of someone else's reality. Become a walking question, and you can then consciously choose your path, instead of just existing.

Certainty is the mortal enemy of possibility. If you live life as a question, it opens the door to endless possibility.

As you begin to unravel the knots of early conditioning it can be a bit disorienting, as the ground your life is built on begins to crumble. This is when we start to really wonder who we were born to be; who are we outside of our conditioning? There are many insights into your unique energy that are readily available, like numerology, astrology, personality assessments, I.Q. tests, enneagram, and many others. Start with what you're drawn to, but explore several aspects of your Divine structure. Find the natural pitfalls, as well as the infinite potential that is you. Begin to build a new sense of self around your highest potential.

And now we must ask: *Why* do I need to know myself? Aside from the benefits listed above, knowing yourself is crucial to reach the heart. But *why?* (You're getting good at this game...)

Knowing thyself is the only way to bring yourself into balance. Reaching the heart (center) requires you to balance the physical, emotional, mental, and spiritual bodies, and achieving that is different for everyone. For example, some people need more self-discipline while others need to learn to let go of so much structure. Some people live an emotional existence while others are emotionally distant, requiring opposite remedies to bring them into balance. Only by knowing yourself, including hidden strengths and weaknesses, can you act accordingly to find balance.

This is where dedication comes into the equation. Some folks are naturally introspective and have been asking questions since they first learned to think. Others are just waking up to their own potential, and have to struggle a bit to get used to the idea of questioning everything. There may be some wavering between human conditioning and higher knowledge, but the sooner one commits to the path of self-awareness, the easier life becomes. The only person that will be with you your whole life is you. Get to know you.

"Self-awareness is not self-centeredness,
and spirituality is not narcissism.
'Know thyself' is not a narcissistic pursuit."
~ Marianne Williamson

MEDITATION

Meditation is absolutely essential to spiritual development. Before you shrug your shoulders and decide it's not your thing, let's talk about what meditation actually means. The very word generally conjures images of yogis dressed in robes, sitting completely still for hours on end, thinking of nothing. Well, that is one kind of meditation, but most of us just can't stop thinking on command, and that's totally normal.

There are several ways to meditate, and the goal is only to stop the monkey mind from chattering incessantly in our heads. To-do lists, self-deprecating comments, judgments, drama... all that noise! To go from that to having no thoughts at all is asking a bit much, and really the point isn't to stop thinking entirely, just stop the babbling. This can be accomplished in several ways, some of which you may already be doing. Try a few of the options, and see what works for you. We are all different.

Breath Work – Breathing meditations are a great place to start. The very basic technique is to breath in deeply to the count of four, then exhale in four counts, concentrating on the breath and the count. Then you can try inhale, hold, exhale, hold, each for four counts. There is no limit to the breathing meditations you can find online. My personal favorite is from Kundalini yoga, called Shabad Kriya. Just look up breath meditation, or take a class on breath work at your local yoga studio. Conscious breathing is a sacred practice by itself, and can lead to a deep meditative state.

Moving Meditation – This is usually done with walking and counting steps, or synchronizing the step and the breath, but it can be any movement. For some, the mind automatically empties when engaged in a physical activity, like swimming, running, or biking. For me, dance (especially ballet) is very meditative. I start to move with the music, and my mind thinks of nothing but the steps... no chattering monkey mind at all, just becoming the movement.

Working Meditation – I call this puttering. Sometime it is easiest to clear the mind by concentrating on tasks. Do some gardening, some light housecleaning. Some people get very frustrated with "chores", but others can get lost in the moment if their hands are busy. Some days this works well for me, other days not so much. Do you "putter" to calm down? It can be quite meditative.

Guided Meditation – Another of my favorites. Here you take a little mental journey, guided by yourself or someone else. Again, there are many options online. I recommend starting with something about 5-15 minutes long, and working your way up when you feel ready. If it gets too long, you will either want to sleep, or your mind will begin to start chattering again. My favorite is the Unity Breath meditation, which unites heaven and Earth in your heart.

Tips – No matter what type of meditation you do, it takes dedication and practice to improve... set aside time, at least twice a week, to quiet the mind. No matter how long you have practiced meditation, some days will be better than others, and that's normal. If you are meditating with your eyes closed, always be sitting or standing upright (no lying down), because of magnetic alignment. Keep your eyes still even when closed (focused up and in, for example)... as the eyes wonder, so does the mind. If meditating to music, pick something soft without words to allow your consciousness to go beyond the limits of language.

Try a few different ways to meditate to find one that works for you, and then dedicate yourself to a practice. In time, the chattering monkey mind learns to relinquish control to your Higher Mind. This is key to awareness and spiritual development.

"By means of a diversion we can avoid our own company 24 hours a day."
~ Pascal

"The question isn't whether the glass is half-empty or half-full, rather do you know how to fill it back up?"
~ Eve Hogan

ESOTERIC POWER

Esoteric power is a bit of an oxymoron, because "power" is a concept of the ego, and the real esoteric juice is from the Spirit. By the way, until you've done enough inner work (ego taming) to be really familiar with the fact that you are not your ego, this discussion will make no sense at all. If that's the case, I invite you to revisit this topic a little later in your journey.

Our symbol here will be a clear drinking glass. When you are born, it is filled with mostly clear water (representing Spirit), and topped off with a layer of oil (representing ego). As you develop through age 14 (or as long as 21), the glass exchanges water for oil (due to programming and conditioning), until it's about 50-50, half Spirit half ego. As an adult you choose to add more water, add more oil, or just go with what you have at that point. Most people just go with what they have, because changing what's in the glass takes applied awareness. Keep in mind, the glass only holds 100%, so to add more Spirit, you must reduce the amount of ego. You can't expand the glass.

True power (for lack of a better term) comes from the Spirit. The pure, clear water in our analogy is pure energy from Source. The more you can remove the ego, the more Spirit you can hold. The ideal situation is to return to the state you were born in, with only a thin film of ego on top of this clear water of Spirit. It isn't that the ego is bad in any way, only that it is, by its very nature, limiting. You need an ego to direct personal will, but if there is too much, it limits the amount and flow of Spirit.

Another important layer of this analogy is in the substances. If you spill water, it just leaves a clean spot when you wipe it up; if you spill oil, it can take a long time to clean. You can easily see through clear water, but looking through oil is extremely distorting, or even impossible. The list goes on. The ego is a necessary part of living in this world, but true potential lives in the Spirit.

This does provide a nice fail-safe to power, though. It is only the ego that is interested in power and control, but to reach the highest power potential, most of the ego must be rejected from the glass, thus limiting the amount of power available to the ego-bound. I'm not saying people with a strong ego-need for power can't harness and direct esoteric power, only that there is much more esoteric power available to those who make room for it by giving up the ego. Good always wins, simply because of this.

In spiritual alchemy, adultery is defined as the mixing of the Spirit and the ego. This is perhaps the greatest esoteric danger. At some point on the path, the initiate will begin to feel the influx and flow of Spirit, and may easily mistake it as their own power, which activates the ego. This is where people get pulled to the dark side, this is the sin of adultery. That is why humility is so greatly emphasized in true Mystery School teachings. Spiritual power flows through you, not from you. Taking ownership of this energy is both limiting and dangerous.

Luckily, most people never feel even a glimmer of this power until they have done much work with their ego, and are on a path to truly know themselves. True esoteric power is limitless, but we can only access that potential as a conduit, not a vessel. When we are willing to let spirit flow through us, without ownership, we can experience the power of the cosmos. Welcome to the initiated.

TEACHERS, MENTORS, AND GURUS

The importance of a teacher or mentor can't be overstated. The Mystery Schools are less about the doctrine, and all about the vibration. Teachers of the Mysteries hold that vibration, and can take you there with them. Yes, it is absolutely possible to find the way on your own, but having someone guide you into that space will increase your learning curve dramatically. Conversely, you need to do your own inner work to be able to return to that space on your own.

I have personally studied under five different Mystery Schools over the years, and they all are meant to raise your vibration. They each have a unique way of doing so, with their own background story, but it's the higher vibration that counts. Like angels & demons? Study with the Golden Dawn. Like inter-dimensional travel? Study the Merkabah. They both end up with the Great White Brotherhood & Sisterhood of Light, but with very different stories to get you there. Just shop around until you find a story you resonate with, or in my case, do several and focus on the parts that serve you.

A teacher holds that high vibrational space for you, while passing on the stories and techniques of their School. At least, while they're teaching. Please remember we are all human, and prone to normal human "stuff" when off duty. When a teacher is in that teaching space, it is mostly channeled information, so they may not ever remember what they said the next day. This happens to me with much of my writing. People will compliment me on a certain writing, and I will have to go reread it to figure out what they're referencing.

Finding a teacher, in my experience, is impossible. In

my life, I have spent hours on the Internet trying to find someone to no avail, but as soon as I dedicate myself to my own spiritual practice, my vibration rises and a teacher pops up out of nowhere. It's magic. Actually, it's a matter of vibration and your own preparation. Finding a REAL teacher is another thing. There are many articles on how to spot a fraud, so I won't repeat that information here. How I tell is by how much I remember after a class. If you are truly in a vibration higher than your normal, memory is almost impossible without notes. Even staying awake can be a challenge. There are other, more practical recommendations, but this one is never mentioned for some reason. I truly believe the vibration of the Mystery Schools will eventually be transmitted to the student via eye contact. At that point, a teacher will be essential, but we aren't there just yet.

The other important point is that a good teacher wants you to succeed on your own, they aren't just gathering followers. They are showing you the vibration you're aiming for, in the hopes you will be able to hold it on your own, and maybe even eventually guide others there. It isn't an easy job to hold that space for others, but the more teachers we have, the easier it becomes, and more lives can be transformed. Just being in that higher vibration changes you.

"Only one person in a million becomes enlightened without a teacher's help."
~ Bodhidharma

THE HEART

The problem is that we are limited by language. Language is only a group of verbal symbols used to describe an experience. This whole system becomes convoluted when people start describing different experiences using the same word. For example, love. You always have to define what you mean, because love comes in many forms and experiences.

We normally use the word heart as an emotional icon (brokenhearted, wearing your heart on your sleeve, etc.), but for the purpose of this discussion, the heart is NOT associated with emotion; emotional experience belongs to the emotional body. Any idea of pain or turmoil involves the emotional body, not the heart. For this discussion, the heart is the center of your being, the void of creation.

The heart is not mental, but it receives intuition. The heart is not emotional, but it pours out unconditional love. The heart is not only physical or spiritual, but where divinity meets matter, and the spark of Life is safely held in the body of Creation.

The point of the Mystery School Teachings is to bring us to more heart-centered living, living in complete balance between physical, mental, emotional (astral), and spiritual bodies. Even understanding what that means can take years, and developing a heart-centered life requires constant vigilance, because we are prone to being thrown off balance simply by living in this world. Just watch the nightly news and you can feel your heart constrict.

Just being aware of what opens your heart and what constricts it is more than half the battle. Awareness is key.

As you sort through your life to find what opens your heart there will be many adjustments, both big and small. Maybe getting a different sounding alarm clock will start your day off more peacefully. Maybe getting a divorce, though tumultuous while in process, will free your heart to open more fully. Like everything, it's different for everyone, and only you know what is best for you and your heart.

The heart is truly the void of creation, and we manifest our lives through an open heart. You know that really happy friend you have, who always seems to be extra "lucky"? That's a perfect example of how an open heart allows all kinds of unexpected wonderfulness to enter your reality. You know that really grumpy friend you have, who always seems to be "unlucky"? Neither one is actually "creating" anything, but their vibration attracts similar vibrations. Creation requires an open heart, always. The only challenge to this game, and it is definitely a challenge, is keeping your heart open to the flow of the Universe.

A quick note about another misunderstood concept: karma. The common understanding of karma is as a punitive system based on punishments and rewards, when it is actually just a vibration. This is what all the Law of Attraction stuff is about. If a person is producing the frequency of anger, they will naturally find people producing a similar frequency to perpetuate that vibration. Nothing here has been created, as this cycle is usually subconscious. Nor has anything been judged and punished. It is simply like attracting like. If you consciously raise your vibration, you will automatically begin to attract people and situations that match. This is a step in the right direction, but it isn't yet creation.

So how does one open the heart? We don't. We can't make it open, we can only encourage and allow, and it opens when it's ready. What we can do is prepare a safe space to allow it to blossom.

Balance your bodies (physical, emotional, mental, spiritual) - Deal with your shadows so your bodies are comfortable and cared for.

Meditate – There are many kinds of meditation. Find one that works for you and dedicate yourself to a practice. Some days will be better than others, and that's ok.

Gratitude – Practicing gratitude is one of the best ways to strengthen spiritual muscle, and open the heart.

Be gentle with yourself – Always. Dedicated, but not hard on yourself. Loving yourself may be the greatest challenge, with the greatest reward.

As the heart opens, information (intuition) pours in, and unconditional love pours out. No expectation, no attachment, as those come from the mental or emotional bodies. You start receiving empathic information from people you may not even know. You start falling deeply in love with random people, animals, and trees. Honestly, it's a bit overwhelming and awkward at first, but eventually you wouldn't have it any other way.

THE GREAT WORK

Many Mystery Schools talk about the Great Work without much definition or guidance. It alludes to doing good deeds, and generally being nice, with the aim of bringing more Light to humanity. All true, but I love directness. We simply aren't in a situation to wonder around the edges, so let's get right down to it.

SPOILER WARNING
Stop reading if you really want to figure
this out on your own!

The Great Work is... (drum roll)... YOU. Ego work, shadow work, fighting your personal demons, however you put it, it's all about self-mastery. Your spiritual spark has already reached (or was created from) the level of immortality through unconditional love, but the human ego is what keeps us from having that experience in body, both individually and collectively.

As you unravel the layers of your psyche, you begin to understand how truly fluid they are. You can completely remake yourself, if you are willing to do so. This is where the work part comes in – training your ego to be willing to change. We get so very attached to our stories that we soon forget they are only stories, and that we can swap them out like changing clothes. Of course, you may need to reevaluate your whole wardrobe (friends, work, lifestyle choices) to make a lasting change, but things are actually meant to change. Everything is either in a state of growth or decay at all times.

The ego provides the illusion of separation on a personal level, just as time and space do on a dimensional level. That's its job. Seeing beyond that veil is our job. The difference is in seeing the world as your ego, or as an observer of your ego. Living as an observer is always a dance, because being pulled into ego drama is just part of life, but pulling yourself back out is the Great Work, and it lasts a lifetime (or a few).

A note of caution on spiritual bypassing – constantly engaging in your own growth is the goal here, not detachment. Pretending nothing gets under your skin, constantly kicking people out of your life to avoid conflict, or assuming it is always someone else's issue, are all forms of spiritual bypassing – avoidance and detachment. The Great Work requires such a deep level of honesty and openness, with yourself first, that most people simply can't manage it. That is why it is set-aside for Initiates... it is a great amount of work.

And why would we come to this beautiful planet just to work the whole time? Divine Union. True love. And here's the catch – it doesn't involve anyone else. True Divine Union happens when your very own Spirit descends fully into your body (and consciousness). I can already hear the questions... Why isn't it here now? How can I be alive without my Spirit in my body? Think of it this way... your Spirit is so big and amazing, it can animate your body by only putting in its pinky toe, and that's all most people will ever experience. Why? There just isn't room with all that ego in the way. The Great Work is making room for your Spirit. YOU are the Great Work. YOU can bring the full Light of your Spirit into manifestation. The work is truly Great.

As above, so below; as within, so without. As each of us engage in this Great Work, the world changes around us. Not only do our perceptions change, but the people we talk to change. Energy flows, and when you are filled with Light, it seeps from every cell. Change yourself, and change the world, literally. Bless you on your path, and may your work be constant.

"The secret of life is in the shadows and not in the open sun; to see anything at all, you must look deeply into the shadow of a living thing."
                                        ~ Ute Saying

"Be the change you wish to see in the world."
                                        ~ Gandhi

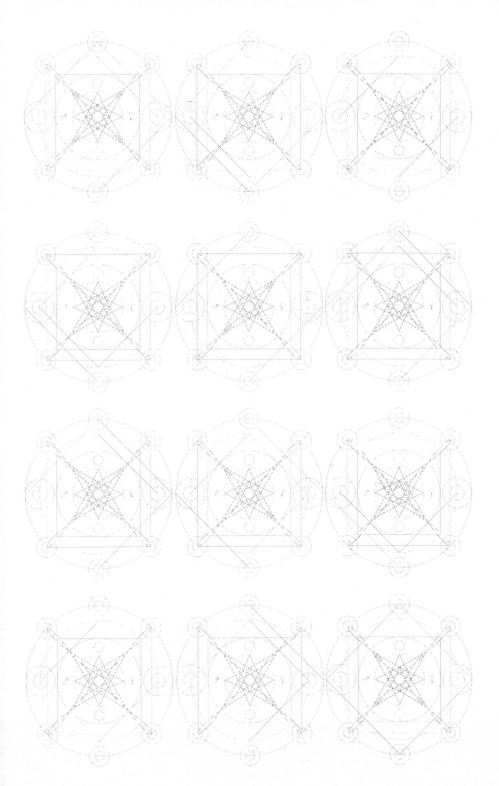

RETURN OF THE GODDESS

CHAPTER 6

~ Second Twin Flame ~
Part I

This story has to be told in parts because it is still unfolding before me, with all the mystery, magic, and terror of any twin flame encounter.

After the whole experience with the void, I was looking for some direction. Something lies beyond, obviously, because I was still breathing. Kabbalah drew my attention, because they speak of crossing the abyss through a kind of death, and resurfacing on the other side. It seemed like these teachings might actually account for the void, and serve as a guideline for post-void recovery, if there were such a thing. I enrolled in an online class that began in January 2012.

It soon became obvious I had chosen the wrong school

(too analytical, no applied mysticism), and I decided to end my studies with them. They had a private Facebook page, and there were five people I enjoyed talking with, so they joined my personal friend list.

Steve was among these five. I recognized him as a kindred soul from his first post, but that isn't unusual for me. Shortly after I left the Kabbalah group, I spent three nights journeying to hang out with someone I didn't recognize. I journey at night occasionally, but never by conscious choice. I get pulled out to do whatever work comes up, but never just to chat, and never three nights in a row. At one point on the second night I asked whom I was visiting and clearly heard Steve. Now that's weird. I thought about asking him if he remembered anything about the journey, but decided it was strange even for me, so I just tried to ignore it... because that works, right?

A couple months later, I started waking up in the middle of the night, usually for three nights in a row, with the feeling that Steve was in danger and I needed to help him. Now, I sometimes dream about people who are calling for help, and I contact them, and the dreams stop. Maybe we chat a bit, maybe I do some energy work, we both feel better, and I can sleep properly again. By itself, this isn't a big deal. But I'd never met Steve in person, or even messaged him privately. That's going to be a fun message: "I know you don't really know me, but I keep dreaming about you. I promise I'm not a stalker, I just want some uninterrupted sleep." Nice. After three months of this monthly sleep disruption pattern, that's pretty much what I wrote to him.

He actually took it quite well, as he has all my insanity since then, but was resistant to letting me do energy work at that point. So we continued this way for another six months, disrupting my sleep and writing to him in support, and the whole time I'm thinking *I must have been this guy's mother in our last life. I am way too concerned with his wellbeing.* In July 2013 he finally let me do the energy work that usually realigns people enough that I stop dreaming about them. *Thank Goddess! I'm finally done here!* Famous last words. I had a couple more dreams about him, but it was definitely better, and by this time we had become friends, so it wasn't quite so weird.

I had put the whole thing to rest in my mind, until late January 2014. I was driving along singing (poorly), and suddenly I'm talking to Steve. *That's random*, I thought, and just let it go. The next week I was grocery shopping and I'm suddenly talking to him again. Literally, my mind went from the shopping list to a full-blown conversation about quitting smoking. Huh. I don't even smoke. Does he? After I got back to my car, I thought about how that happened. The only other time I experience anything like that is when I speak telepathically with Adriane, my sister twin flame.

I emailed Steve to see if he was aware of the conversations, and though he was aware they happened, he thought he was just talking to himself, not to me. I supplied the details of the conversations, so he would know we were talking telepathically. He asked how this happens, and I'm pretty sure I said, "I don't fucking know!" I still hadn't recognized him as a twin flame, but the weirdness could no longer be denied.

A few weeks later I invited Steve to an online class by Drunvalo Melchizedek (the modern father of Merkabah teachings), but he couldn't attend. I was already trained as a Merkabah teacher, so I offered to teach him myself, and after thinking it over, he said he was ready. This was our first voice contact. Turns out, voice contact is almost as powerful as eye contact for twins, whether you recognize them or not. The training went fine, and I don't know that he felt anything at all, but my world shifted dramatically. I was talking to Adriane about how my love for him kept intensifying (the unconditional kind not the romantic kind) like a pure white and gold cord from my heart to his. In her infinite wisdom, she told me to just feel what I feel. Quite possibly the best and most destructive advice I've ever received. So the next time I meditated, I did just that: opened up fully to that love.

Holy shit.

It was like every cell in my body was filled with light, like I was breathing for the first time. In hindsight, I'd call it a Kundalini awakening, and it left me in a state of total bliss for at least two weeks. After I came down from the bliss-trip, I did a lot of reading and found that most of my experiences were typical of twin flames. Now I knew who he was on a soul level, but still had no indication of the role he would play in this life... Brother? Lover? Friend? All that mattered to me was that deep, unconditional love.

After I recognized him as a twin, things got really strange, as if they weren't already. Yes, my experience of Steve is right at the top of my "weird shit" list. Our emotional bodies merged, so I could feel everything he was feeling. I was a Vulcan and he was a Drama Queen. It sucked. I completely lacked the skill set to handle that level of emotion. But at the same time, the world took on a dimension of beauty and wonder that I had never experienced before. Emotion... who knew? I always thought it just looked messy. And then there were the past life dreams and visions, the abrupt increase in intuition, and the random bursts of energy in different chakras. 2014 was a wild ride.

The most profound and lasting part of the whole thing is this upgrade to my heart chakra. I used to be able to love unconditionally, in a limited scope, but normally my love was conditional: I love you like a friend, or like a lover, or like a child, always using some category. Now, my heart is just open or closed, on or off. I completely fall in love with strangers, animals, and random trees. I feel like I live in a Rumi poem. There's just no explaining that one.

I kept checking with Steve to see what was happening on his end, but he didn't go though all this. He has always met my insanity with warmth and compassion, though I'm pretty sure there were times he was quite thankful we live 2000 miles apart. Having someone you've never met declare their undying love for you can't be easy to accept. Sometimes I wonder if he actually got the harder job by not recognizing me. It was definitely more work to hold the emotional body for both of us. Vulcan is so much easier.

Does it matter that he didn't share this experience? Not at all. It has forever changed me and my course in life, and for that I am eternally grateful. For the first time ever I am happy to be alive. Not that I was unhappy before, just that now I feel like life is an adventure, instead of just a mission. The world is beautiful and the possibilities are endless. Joining that Kabbalah class to recover from the void was exactly what I needed to do, though the remedy came from this twin experience, not the teachings. I feel like I have been drawn back into my body.

So where are we now, at the start of 2015? Right where we need to be, I'm sure. I still haven't met Steve in person, though we talk regularly, and he seems to have accepted the undying love part. I still feel his ups and downs, but not so dramatically. And most importantly, that heart link is bright and shiny and full of love. I still don't know the roles we will play in this life, but we're building a fabulous friendship, which is always the best place to start.

To be continued...

"A love story, at least a convincing one, requires three elements - the lover, the beloved, and the adventures they have together."
~ Jane Smiley

"Every love story is beautiful, but ours is my favorite."
~ Unknown

RETURN OF THE GODDESS

There has been much talk about the Divine Feminine, or return of the Goddess. I was expecting a very gentle, nurturing energy to enter human consciousness. Not so much. As a friend said, "She's back, and She's pissed!" I don't think I quiet agree with that sentiment, but She is definitely stronger, more defined, and more insistent than I ever imagined feminine energy could be. I think this says way more about my ignorance of what it means to be truly feminine than it does about the energy itself. What is feminine energy, anyway? The way I was raised, femininity was never held in high regard, and that message is echoed throughout our society.

First, we need to understand this isn't a gender thing. All humans have both masculine and feminine energy within them, and we can have an imbalance in one or both of them, regardless of our human gender. The phenomenon we are calling 'Return of the Goddess' is really just a return to balance within ourselves, and then expressing that new balance in society. Not only have we been heavily emphasizing the masculine (lots of doing and getting, as opposed to being and nurturing), but we have also been living mostly in the shadow side of both energies.

For example, the shadow of the masculine can be aggressive or an eternal child (Peter Pan complex), among other things. The feminine shadow can include manipulation and victimization (martyr complex). Again, this is NOT about gender. I know lots of women with control issues (masculine imbalance) and lots of men who live as victims (feminine imbalance). When in balance, masculine energy can be protective without being possessive, focused without being dominating; feminine energy can be nurturing without being smothering, creative without being flighty. It's a matter of balance, as well as living in the light instead of the shadow.

Masculine energy is what our world is currently built on. It's an outward moving force, yang energy, with the emphasis on doing and acquiring. It's a mental energy, and likes step-by-step processes. It's about focusing the will, and making things happen. It's a linear energy, and is represented by a straight line.

Feminine energy is largely missing from our current culture, thus the Return of the Goddess to bring us back into balance. It's an inward force, yin energy, with the emphasis on being and nurturing. It's a feeling energy, and likes spontaneity. It's about allowing life to flow, and surrender to Divine Will. It is a cyclical energy, and it represented by a circle or spiral.

What does all this mean? It means we are being nudged (some harder than others) to return to balance. How does it look? Honestly, it looks like chaos and feels even worse. Being a recovering control freak, there are many days I simply can't find the beauty in this Divine dance, can't find my place in this new world. Other days I feel so blessed to be here to witness this shift humanity is making. For me, allowing the feminine energy to flow through me, no matter what my mental to-do list says, makes the process easier. For others, taking action towards a goal might be beneficial. We are each being brought into balance in whatever way we need.

Have you felt this strange pull to be you in an entirely new way? Don't fight it. In my experience, resistance is futile. Give yourself permission to change. That's harder than it sounds, because we've spent years creating our identities, and we get rather attached to our stories. The energy around you is changing, the collective consciousness is shifting. Accepting this change will be the beginning of a whole new adventure for us all.

"In all the great religious systems, there are divine beings who represent the feminine face of the divine."
~ Marianne Williamson

"Mysteries are feminine; they like to veil themselves but still want to be seen and divined."
~ Karl Wilhelm Friedrich Schlegel

COLLECTIVE MISOGYNY

Misogyny is a hatred of women, but I want to expand the conversation to include all things of feminine energy, specifically the physical world. All things have both masculine and feminine energy. The masculine energy (spirit) combines with the feminine energy (matter) to create our physical existence. The illusion of separation is strong (fall from grace), thanks to our egos so masterfully holding the veil, but I assure you, both energies are fully present.

Somewhere along the way, we started blaming the physical (feminine) for this sense of separation from Source (masculine). Did the Yahweh cult begin misogyny, or did our collective misogyny birth this cult? Interesting question, but the bigger concern is where we are now, and how to correct the thinking. Women as a gender aren't really the issue, it's our loathing of the physical world, right down to our own bodies.

We are all homesick due to the illusion of separation, and it makes sense that we would innately want to shuffle loose the mortal coil to get back home, but then why did we leave? The physical isn't all that bad of an experience, until you forget it's just an experience and start to believe it is reality. Several thousand years ago we forgot. Ascetic spiritual practices started popping up, to lessen the grip of the body (self-inflicted torture, really), and punish the body for leading us astray with the pleasure of the senses. So the physical part was fun, and that was the problem. This belief was quickly applied to sex, and the mixture of masculine and feminine energy (similar to our own creation) was restricted, regulated, and generally held in low regard. Like sex was a symbol of our original fall from grace.

First it was women, then the senses, now even our planet is being abused to satisfy this primal idea that being in body is the reason we feel so far from the Divine. While we loathe life, we also fear death, having suppressed the circular pattern of mortality. And if you look at how you regard your own body (feminine energy), you may be shocked at how deep the misogyny goes. Do you complain about pollution of our planet while eating fast food, drinking soda or alcohol, or smoking? Do you enjoy physical highs (sex, food, coffee) but loath caring for your body with healthy food and exercise? When you're physically sick or tired, do you lovingly care for yourself, or are you angry that you can't do what you had planned for the day? So many daily examples of our general disgust with the physical experience.

The entire physical world is all the same energy, the Divine Feminine: Your body, the plants, the animals, and the Earth itself.

We all know our current system is based on masculine energy – personal will over intuition, doing over being, conquering over nurturing. We have been taught from birth to ignore our bodies and emotions (body chemicals), and to create our lives with the mind and will power. Our bodies are to be conquered and held in submission to our will, or to be exploited for sensory amusement and gratification. It's no wonder the whole thing is crashing down, being that it requires both polarities to exist.

Awareness is everything. Really consider how you treat your body. For most people, it's either a trashcan or an amusement park. Then look around you at the planet – pollution, environmental disasters, factory farms, GMO crops, the list goes on. See the correlation? If you want to save the Earth, start with being aware and adjusting your own attitude about your body, your own Divine Feminine. This isn't a pep talk about body confidence, this is pointing out that the physical is *literally* one thing, it's fractal. Be a good steward to your own personal Gaia.

This is why the body is the Temple of the Soul – it is the container holding the Spirit. There is no separation. Loving our physical selves brings us into our bodies, which is where we are in touch with what we remember as home. It is where we can feel that original Divine Union, instead of the veil of separation. Treat your body with love and respect, as it is a Divine creation, just like the Earth. Your attitude towards the physical will become increasingly important as we strive for energetic balance and union in 2016-2017.

"Remember, your body is a temple, not a 7-Eleven."
~ Jennifer Love Hewitt

"Cherish sunsets, wild creatures and wild places.
Have a love affair with the wonder
and beauty of the earth."
~ Stewart Udall

MASCULINE POWER

It looks outwardly that men have all the power: Male dominant social structure with the focus on mental achievement, conquest (money and sex), and accumulation. It seems like balancing power just means men need to relax and learn to share. There's another side. As men have overtly controlled women, women have covertly been emasculating men.

I am using gender terms for simplicity, but the roles can easily be reversed, as we all have both masculine and feminine energy within us.

The aggressive male is outdated at this point. Yes, there is still plenty of abuse going on, but it's been brought into the spotlight as a bad thing. What's far more common at this point is the eternal child, or refusal to grow up. Why? Because society has accepted that it's fine to steal boys' power from the get-go. "Boys develop slower. You know how boys are," and it continues into adolescence with "they're just being boys" and into marriage with all the nagging because "men are such children." We take away their power by repeatedly telling them they aren't strong enough to handle life because they are "just boys", and hoping they will marry "a good woman" to take care of them, being that they are incapable of taking care of themselves.

This is played out in relationships as the woman constantly nagging and belittling her husband, while he silently gets angry and passive-aggressive. Instead of being raised to be whole independent people, women are taught they need a man for financial security, and men are taught they need an eternal mother to take care of them. No wonder relationships are so difficult. We are each wrapped up in controlling the other person's power, instead of balancing our own.

If any of this sounds familiar, start with forgiving yourself and your partner. Most of us were raised with perfect role models of imbalance. And so were our parents. This has been going on for a very long time. As the issue comes into your awareness, you can start the process of change.

If you are a nagger (of either sex) you are trying to control the other person's masculine energy. When you notice yourself starting this old pattern, stop and respect the other person as a capable human being. Let it go. Even if they are going about something in a way you don't understand, just let them do it. If they fail, respect them for trying. Your partner is whole and capable.

If you are always waiting for an eternal mother to guide your every move and keep you safe, remember you are a powerful being. It might be scary at first, to hold your own power, but you won't break. We all get bruised up a bit as we learn to fly, but you can handle it. Promise. It's okay to grow up and be strong.

Objectification of women is well publicized and being understood and dealt with in new ways. Let's also examine the emasculation of men, and how to restore their power. We are all coming back into balance.

"Honor is simply the morality of superior men."
~ H. L. Mencken

FINDING BALANCE

I have spent the last two years struggling to understand masculine and feminine energy. Not relationships, or gender, or societal roles, but the combination of Divine Masculine and Divine Feminine that we each carry within us, and how to find balance. I'm one of those people who likes puzzles, and figuring out how things fit together, so I started with reading all kinds of stuff about masculine and feminine energy. What I read simply doesn't mesh with my own experiences and observations, so I'll share my take on the issue.

First, many people are confusing the shadow side of the energies with their true meaning. It is common in this society to see the masculine as aggressive or childish, and the feminine as submissive or manipulative – all of which are shadows of the true energies. There are so many people advocating the strengthening of the feminine by means of weakening the masculine, or using sexuality as a road to power. Not helping... so not helping. (Side note – it angers me greatly to assign submissiveness to the feminine. Receptive yes, but not submissive. I have found nothing but the greatest strength there.)

In my observation, feminine energy isn't some wild, sexual, unpredictable force. Look at the role of a mother... a mother has to create a safe space for her child to grow, and hold that space for years. Before birth, this safe space is the womb. There is nothing unpredictable about her constant nurturing, and holding that space is essential to raising healthy kids. Look at nature... it isn't random, scattered, unpredictable, or even that creative (in the spontaneous way). Nature is an incredibly well organized and reliable system. It may look wild and dangerous on the surface, but the entire ecosystem is amazingly structured, if you actually study it. In my book, feminine energy is about boundaries, holding space, and nurturing.

They are a bit closer with the masculine side, saying it is a direct and focused energy. From what I can tell, the masculine is all about expansion and creation, in a direct and focused way. If it is left to its own devises, it will just keep expanding without limit, which has resulted in conquest and greed, never having enough. Inwardly, rampant masculine energy results in a constant feeling of unrest, of never being quite satisfied, or quite good enough.

The balance, then, is firm boundaries creating a safe, nurturing space to hold the drive and expansion in a secure and positive way. This applies to microcosm and macrocosm... Just think on this a bit.

Now there is the issue of a third energy. Many attribute this spontaneous, playful energy to the repressed feminine, but I disagree. This is definitely a separate energy. I believe it is the Divine Child, the creation of Divine Masculine and Divine Feminine working in perfect balance. This energy is playful, curious, unpredictable, joyful, and full of wonder. As we balance our masculine and feminine, it creates this amazing Divine Child energy. This is the space we are yearning for, and it is available inside each of us, as we balance our energies.

As we come into balance and allow the creation of the Divine Child within, we can also create this same balance and wonder in our outer world.

So how can you balance? Be aware of your world, both inner and outer. Having good boundaries is an issue for many right now, understandably so. We feel guilty, or selfish, or unworthy of having boundaries. This is your Divine Feminine energy; allow it to help you create a sacred and nourishing space to grow from. This will allow your Divine Masculine to bring you direction and drive, within that safe space. The joy that follows is the birth of your Divine Child. And this, my friends, is magic... and the beginning of a new world.

"There is an invisible strength within us;
when it recognizes two opposing objects of desire,
it grows stronger."
~ Rumi

"Your task is not to seek for love,
but merely to seek and find all the
barriers within yourself that
you have built against it."
~ Rumi

BE YOU

CHAPTER 7

~ The Prophecy ~

Almost everyone knows a few details surrounding their conception or birth. My Grandma once told me she always expected my uncle to be a sailor, because he was conceived in the bathtub. Seriously. Why would your granddaughter need to know that? But the story surrounding my birth is pretty fabulous, if I do say so myself.

Before she ever met my father, my Mom had a dream about having a child. She was to give birth to someone who was going to start a new religion, and end the current beliefs. When she met my Dad she recognized him immediately, not by his appearance, but by his energy. She got pregnant, out of wedlock, and told Grandma about the dream, stating she had to keep the baby. She worked hard on picking a name with the appropriate numerology, and settled on Nathan James. Natha Jane was the best she could do on short notice. It has better numerology, anyway.

Grandma was a devout Jehovah's Witness, and wasn't pleased about this prophetic dream. She used to tell me, "Do you know why you're a girl? It's because I prayed every night of your Mom's pregnancy that you would be a girl and break the prophecy." Not only was I born female, I had red hair and brown eyes, just like Grandma always wanted one of her girls to have. Between the two, she welcomed me joyfully, even out of wedlock.

The best part is that Mom never dreamed about the gender of the child, she just assumed it would need to be a boy to be a religious leader. She confided this to me, but she never corrected Grandma. It was better to let her believe she broke a prophecy.

Isn't that a fun story?

*"Whatever we expect with confidence
becomes our own self-fulfilling prophecy."*
~ Brian Tracy

BE YOU

Everyone is born of great potential with unique gifts to share with the world, and then we are loaded up like a pack mule with other people's baggage. We are conditioned with behavior patterns and social norms, until we totally forget the point of being us. Such a waste.

Even after you do all the deep, shadow work to gain access to your birthright, it still may be a struggle to completely come out of the Lightworker closet. There are ancient and archetypal fears about being seen. You may actually have memories of being burned at the stake. The Witch Wound is real, and many of us run headlong into that wall. I argued with my guides for about a year before I began writing, because it felt dangerous to really be who I am.

Astrological Ages change about every 2000 years. In 2012, we went from the Age of Pisces to the Age of Aquarius. Pisces was all about conformity, and social norms governing individual decisions. Fitting in was the way to go. Aquarius is about serving the collective with your individual gifts. Be totally you, and we all benefit. The collective is stronger with each different string in the tapestry. We are transitioning these two forces, so we feel the influence of both Ages.

Every time one of us steps up to our destiny, it makes it easier for the next. This is not only leading by example, it's actually quickening the shift of vibration. More than ever before, your actions affect the collective.

As Joseph Campbell says, follow your bliss. Find what brings you to that place of joy, and offer your gifts to the world. This makes all the difference. Your unique gifts make this tapestry beautiful and whole. Be you.

TRUST & OPENNESS

In the new paradigm, we will be living with open hearts, which leads to awareness, empathic abilities, and eventually telepathy. Science and technology are simply a reflection (or manifestation) of collective human consciousness. Social media and instant communication are preparing us for the transparency of the future. It will be tough to keep secrets when we are all telepathic. And good luck hiding your energy.

At first, this idea may make you feel naked and exposed, wanting to retreat into a cave where no one can "read" you. We all like to think we are our own, and we are, but there is a collective heartbeat growing. We can only win this game with unity, and learning to open up to others is really just unlearning all the ideas of needing protection. All of us have felt threatened in this world, in one way or another. The threats are real, I get it, but true strength comes from overcoming them within. If you were abused as a child, have the courage to face that experience, and then release it to the past where it belongs. Keeping your armor on when the fight is over is just heavy and exhausting. Release the layers that no longer serve you.

As with everything, openness and trust begin within. Can you really be open to all your own aspects without judgment? Can you look at your life without berating yourself? I think being fully open and accepting with ourselves may be the hardest step in the process. Removing negative self-talk is a never ending process, but necessary, and completely worth the effort.

Build trust within by allowing yourself to be human, with all the flaws and quirks we all have, but without judging. As you begin to accept these 'human moments', you will be able to open more fully to yourself. Leave the criticism behind, and just be wherever you are. The more accepting and compassionate you are to yourself, the more open you become. Trust builds.

Until we are comfortable facing all parts of our own psyche, there will be fear in letting others truly see us. Know thyself. Do your shadow work. Bring light and love to your darkest recesses, and there will no longer be room for fear. People are already reading you, just as you are reading them, it's just becoming a conscious process.

The world needs your open heart.

"Let my soul smile through my heart and my heart smile through my eyes, that I may scatter rich smiles in sad hearts."
~ Paramahansa Yogananda

"Wherever you go, go with all your heart."
~ Confucius

INTIMACY AND CONNECTION

This topic is so complex, yet so simple. Let's start with the human layer, and work our way up.

As humans, we have been taught that love is about attachment, expectation, and condition. It is totally true that we need boundaries in this dimension, to protect both body and ego. This is where love gets confusing. Most people equate unconditional love with lack of boundaries. Worst case "I know my partner abuses me sometimes, but I love them, so I will stay and just forgive them." Wrong. So wrong, on so many levels.

Loving someone unconditionally, in human terms, simply means you want him or her to reach their highest potential, even if you can no longer be in their life. It is about encouraging and supporting them, even from afar. Actually, it is often easier to love unconditionally from afar, because the boundary issue isn't as noticeable. Boundaries are vital for healthy relationships.

Most people talk about love, when they really mean attachment. They are attached to a story, or a life style, or most often, to a chemical reaction. "I love you" usually means "I love the body high I get when I'm near you." This is the butterflies and fireworks of falling in love. It's a fabulous feeling, but it isn't love. It fades, people wonder where the spark went, and move on to the next relationship. True love would ask what serves you both best, not where did the spark go.

Our evolution to the 5th dimension requires a shift in our ability to truly love. Most people are tired of the fireworks without any deep connection. True intimacy is a soul-level thing, and is becoming more available, and required. People want to truly connect. As we become more of a collective, this connection will be more natural.

This is a big part of the reason there have been so many relationship issues since 2012. We need deeper connections, and the very nature of relationships is changing. The goal used to be to get married, have kids, and stay married to that same person until death. Then divorce became the norm. Now, it's just chaos out there, operating under the guise of polyamory and tantra. (Side note: True polyamory isn't just sleeping around, and true tantra isn't about having better orgasms.) People are searching for true connection, in the most intimate way they know how.

The thing is, the depth of connection people are searching for isn't found in sex. Yes, you can add sex to that connection, but the intimacy is elsewhere. The intimacy people really want is to be truly seen, truly heard, and accepted without judgment. Complete healing through connection.

This depth of connection is available to all of us right now, in a variety of simple ways. We can all be a little more real in all our relationships, from lover to the person who bags your groceries. A little more eye contact, a few more questions about their day. With closer friends or partners, try some white tantra, or eye gazing. Simply put the playlist on shuffle and look into each other's eyes for three songs, then talk about the experience.

You have to be willing to be open enough to be seen, as well as see others without judgment. Start small, and be honest. Find a friend who you can invite on this adventure, or connect with a group that does this kind of work. Remember, you can only meet someone as deeply as you have met yourself (and vice-versa), so do your shadow (ego) work to make room for this connection.

These connections are preparing us for what we really want – union with our own Higher Self. That's true Divine Union. Then unconditional Love becomes our playground. Is there anything more intimate than welcoming your own soul?

"To love and be loved is to feel the sun from both sides."
~ David Viscott

"The minute I heard my first love story, I started looking for you, not knowing how blind that was. Lovers don't finally meet somewhere. They're in each other all along."
~ Rumi

REMEMBER

That's all, just remember. Remember where you came from, who you are, and who you were meant to be. We are here to change the world, and we didn't come alone. The Tribe is gathering. Unite and remember.

Two of my favorite books for jogging the memory are:
The Life You Were Born to Live by Dan Millman
Astrology for the Soul by Jan Spiller

I recommend you look at natal astrology (Vedic or Western), and birthdate numerology, before going into personality tests and intuitive readings. Let's face it, most of us can manipulate the questions on a personality test, but there's no changing your birthday. Look at who you were when you got here, not who you've learned to be.

Be curious. Use these tools to discover who came here to be, what gifts you carry, and what challenges you will likely face. No, not all of what you read will resonate, but you will know what parts to keep. I reread these descriptions of me yearly, just to see what's changed in me, and if I am still on path. For me, this has helped immensely, even though my intuition is pretty stellar.

Another great way to jog the memory is time spent with the Others. Find people like you, have conversations, make eye contact. I find large chunks of my memory returning as I do this. Find the Others.

I've never cared for the word 'healing', because it implies you are broken, and need to be fixed. But if we replace 'healing' with 'remembering', it all makes sense. Our greatest healing is really remembering who we are. Mostly remember you hale from the unseen. You are always loved. You are always supported. You are always safe. Remember.

AFTERWORD

Just to tie up a few loose ends...

My life continues to be as strange as ever, although now I prefer to think of it as 'magical'. Sounds better. Nice ring to it.

As of this publishing in late 2016 my ataxia continues to improve, but very slowly. As with any chronic physical issue, there are good days and bad days.

I'm not holding out on you with the Twin Flame story of Steve. We still haven't met in person. Our friendship continues to grow, and we'll meet eventually.

I do plan on future writings. You can also check out my site at www.WalkingInBothWorlds.com for the latest updates.

And most importantly, the Tribe continues to gather. I have met some of the most amazing people along the way, many just in the past couple years. I am so grateful, and truly humbled, to know such amazing souls.

And a special thanks to YOU for joining me on this adventure in time and space. Namaste.

"Set your life on fire. Seek those who fan your flames."
~ Rumi

142

Further Exploration

Books:
The Life You Were Born to Live by Dan Millman
Astrology for the Soul by Jan Spiller
Outrageous Openness by Tosha Silver

Movies:
What the Bleep Do We Know? (2005)

Groups:
AMORC (Ancient Mystical Order of Rosae Crucis)
www.amorc.org or www.rosicrucian.org

The School of Remembering, Drunvalo Melchizedek
www.theschoolofremembering.net

Check www.meetup.com for local spiritual groups.
Be willing to try several, and to move on when you're ready.
Remember, if you are the brightest light in the room, it's
time to find another room.

Blogs & Such:
Me www.WalkingInBothWorlds.com
Lee Harris www.leeharrisenergy.com
Sandra Walter www.sandrawalter.com
Patricia Cota-Robles www.ersofpeace.org